Second Edition

English for Adult Competency

BOOK 1

Autumn Keltner
Leann Howard
Frances Lee

SAN DIEGO COMMUNITY COLLEGE DISTRICT

with Nancy Hampson and Robin Lee

PRENTICE HALL REGENTS
Englewood Cliffs, New Jersey 07632

Editorial/production supervision and
  interior design: Noël Vreeland Carter
Manufacturing buyer: Ray Keating
Cover design: Bruce Kenselaar

Illustrated by Mark Neyndorff

Printed in the United States of America

10 9 8 7 6 5 4 3 2 1

ISBN 0-13-280348-8

Prentice-Hall International (UK) Limited, London
Prentice-Hall of Australia Pty. Limited, Sydney
Prentice-Hall Canada Inc., Toronto
Prentice-Hall Hispanoamericana, S.A., Mexico
Prentice-Hall of India Private Limited, New Delhi
Prentice-Hall of Japan, Inc., Tokyo
Simon & Schuster Asia Pte. Ltd., Singapore
Editora Prentice-Hall do Brasil, Ltda., Rio de Janeiro

CONTENTS

Topics: Greetings, introductions, personal information, forms, states of being, feelings, family, time, months, dates, telephone messages

Functions: Asking for and giving information, describing, inquiring, giving and taking messages

Structures: Present affirmative, negative, interrogative-to be, WH questions, present affirmative, adverbs of frequency, simple future

Life Skill Reading: Forms, messages

Reading Exercise: Personal identification

Topics: Types of stores, foods, prices, comparison shopping, types of packaging, grocery ad, food location, spoiled food, eating out, making change

Functions: Expressing needs, asking for and providing information, comparing, complaining, offering/refusing offers, expressing preferences

Structures: To be-present, comparatives and superlatives, yes/no questions and answers, present, WH questions (what, where, how much/many), may (permission), can (ability)

Life Skill Reading: Prices, grocery ad, food expiration dates, menu

Reading Exercise: Shopping for food

3 HEALTH 43

Topics: External and internal parts of the body, common health problems, reporting school absences, thermometer, appointments, diseases, immunization/vaccination, health form, prescription/non-prescription medicine, dosages, emergency situations

Functions: Asking for, giving, and interpreting information, describing common problems, expressing sympathy, asking for clarification, giving directions, requesting help

Structures: WH questions; to be-present/past, yes/no questions and answers, regular and irregular verbs, present/past, imperative, modals-should, may, can, future contractions-I'll, objective pronouns, tag questions, verb + infinitive, prepositions of place

Life Skill Reading: Thermometer, appointment card, health form, prescription labels

Reading Exercise: Health

4 TRANSPORTATION 68

Topics: Means of transportation, pedestrian safety, directions, riding the bus, using a taxi, full service/self service gas stations, parts of an automobile, road signs, round trip bus trips, lost luggage

Functions: Describing, asking for and giving directions, requesting clarification, requesting service, explaining, requesting information, requesting assistance

Structures: Present affirmative and interrogative, imperative, negative imperative modal-should, WH questions, past affirmative and interrogative

Life Skill Reading: Road signs

Reading Exercise: Transportation

INTRODUCTION

English for Adult Competency, Books 1 and *2* are basic texts for adult students who need to learn the oral language patterns and vocabulary required in day-to-day situations. They provide classroom instructors with materials and activities that are effective and relevant to the real needs of non- and limited-English speaking adults.

Book 1 is intended for adults who have had little or no previous instruction in English and need to develop the listening and speaking skills required to communicate effectively in the following content areas:

    I.   Personal Identification and Communication
   II.   Food
  III.   Health
  IV.   Transportation
   V.   Housing
  VI.   Clothing
 VII.   Looking for and Keeping a Job
VIII.   Banking and Money Orders
  IX.   Community Resources
   X.   United States Historical Holidays

The units are situational and non-sequential with appropriate structures integrated into each lesson. The primary purpose of each lesson is to develop immediately useable oral communication skills. The materials are designed to take the students beyond the level of merely knowing *about* the language and beyond repeating memorized dialogues. Their purpose is, through a variety of student centered activities, to enable the students to *use* language for a real purpose.

Each unit consists of the following:

1. A list of competency objectives
2. Situational or functional dialogues
3. Vocabulary and structure practices
4. Interactive pair practice exercises and/or interview questions
5. Visuals
6. Reading exercises

The performance-based objectives, listed on the first page of each unit, designate functional competencies that students are to achieve. Since the text is designed primarily to develop oral communication skills, demonstrated performance of the competency is stressed. Structures are focused on in the practices following the dialogues. In addition to structures, language functions are also addressed where applicable. The practices and pair practice activities provide opportunities for students to practice the language they will need outside the classroom.

Teaching Guidelines

It is strongly recommended that instructors read through and study each unit before planning instruction. By so doing, the instructor will have a clear idea of the scope of the unit, its goals and objectives, and the activities which draw on students' experiences to introduce, reinforce, and lead to mastery of the competencies identified through ongoing needs assessments.

USING THE VISUALS   Visuals are an integral part of each unit. These adult-oriented pictures add realism and relevance to the lesson and enable beginning students to attach immediate meaning to the situation presented. Use of the visuals can:

1. Set the scene and provide context for the situations in the dialogues. By asking questions about the visuals, the instructor can assess how relevant the situation is to the students' lives and how much language they already have to communicate in a similar situation.
2. Develop the topic concepts for each unit.
3. Provide a concrete link for vocabulary development.
4. Cue responses in pair practice and chart activities.

DIALOGUES   The structural patterns and concepts of each unit are introduced through dialogues which center around a single situational topic. The following steps are recommended in the presentation of a dialogue:

1. *SETTING THE SCENE*   Before presenting the dialogue itself, it is important to set the scene or provide a meaningful context for the students. The instructor can prepare the students by using the visuals in the text to generate a discussion of what the dialogue might be about and what language might be used. The instructor may also describe the situation presented through the dialogue, using the vocabulary necessary for comprehension. By pre-teaching the core vocabulary and expressions, the instructor will ensure that the students are better prepared to comprehend the dialogue in context.

2. *MODELING THE DIALOGUE AND COMPREHENSION CHECK*   Once the scene is set, the instructor models the complete dialogue with books closed. The instructor uses pictures, gestures, pantomime, or whatever is necessary to get the meaning across. If an aide is available, instructor and aide can each take one part of the dialogue. Following the modeling, the instructor asks different types of questions (yes/no, WH questions, etc.) to check student comprehension of the dialogue.

3. *REPETITION OF THE DIALOGUE*   Once the students demonstrate an understanding of the dialogue, the instructor models each line and the students repeat. After repeating all lines of the dialogue, the instructor takes one role (A) and the students take the other (B). Then the roles are reversed for another practice of the dialogue. Next, the instructor divides the class in half. One half assumes

one role, the second half, the other. Finally, pairs of students practice the dialogue, while the instructor circulates, listening for pronunciation or structure problems, offering assistance as needed.

4. *DRILLS* As the instructor is practicing the dialogue, it may become obvious that additional drilling of particular phrases is needed before the dialogue as a whole can be practiced. Four main types of drills are used to prepare students for simple communicative interaction. These four types are repetition, chain, substitution, and transformation drills. They are categorized as mechanical drills in that they are tightly controlled, and there is only one correct response. The purpose of mechanical drills is to lead students to the memorization of basic patterns (structures) in English.

The repetition drill is the most elementary drill; the teacher (T) models, students (SS) or student (S) repeat(s). The teacher must make sure that the students understand what they are repeating and are not merely parroting the teacher. Use of visuals, real objects and/or body language help to ensure comprehension.

In repetition drills the teacher models the pattern several times while the students listen. Then the entire class responds chorally; next, half the class; then one row of students, and finally, individual students respond. If the exchange is question/answer, the teacher models the answer first, then the question.

```
       Example: T:    I need a new shirt
                SS:   I need a new shirt.
                 T:   I need a new shirt.
             ½ SS:    I need a new shirt.
                 T:   I need a new shirt.
        1 row SS:     I need a new shirt.
                 T:   I need a new shirt.
               1S:    I need a new shirt.
```

The same procedure is used for introducing the question, "What do you need?" This question/answer repetition drill leads logically to the introduction of a chain drill. The teacher cues S1 to ask S2 the question; S2 responds and asks S3 the question and so on. Chain drills can be initiated in several parts of the room so that several groups of students are practicing the exchange at one time.

Substitution drills provide additional practice in using structures previously introduced through repetition. However, in substitution drills the student's attention is focused on the substitution item, and the use of the structure becomes automatic. At first, a substitution drill is cued by visuals or objects or body language, and later by oral or written cues.

```
     Example: T:    I have a headache.
              SS:   I have a headache.
               T:   I have a headache (cue: [visual, oral or written] stomachache).
              SS:   I have a stomachache.
               T:   I have a stomachache. (cue: earache)
              SS:   I have an earache.
```

After several structures have been introduced through repetition, chain and/or substitution drills, transformation drills can be used to emphasize a change in the structure.

```
     Example: T:    I have a headache.
              SS:   I have a headache.
               T:   I have a headache.      cue:  he
              SS:   He has a headache.
               T:   He has a headache.      cue:  you
              SS:   You have a headache.
               T:   You have a headache.   cue:  she
              SS:   She has a headache.
```

These four kinds of drills can easily move from the mechanical drill category to meaningful exchanges by encouraging the students to respond from one of several appropriate responses. The response will be real, based on the individual's own situation. When asked, "What do you need?", the student responds based on his/her own personal need—"A pencil," "A notebook," "A paper," "Nothing"—instead of simply reacting to a visual or oral cue.

If students have difficulty repeating a phrase, a "backward buildup" may be used. In backward buildup drills the instructor first models complete sentence, and then proceeds as follows:

Example: T: I have to make an appointment with the doctor.
T: With the doctor
SS: With the doctor
T: An appointment with the doctor
SS: An appointment with the doctor
T: Make an appointment with the doctor
SS: Make an appointment with the doctor
T: I have to make an appointment with the doctor

5. *PRACTICE OF THE DIALOGUE* On subsequent days, further practice of the dialogue can be carried out in small groups or in pairs. Students can begin to generate the dialogue with minimal cues through the provision of pictures or the first few words of each line.

Dialogues are not necessarily designed to be memorized. They are instead a device for developing mastery of language structure and vocabulary while providing a context for relevant topics and situations. The sentences in the dialogue serve as models for practicing and expanding the language and cultural context of the topic. The final and most crucial step is for students to reconstruct the situation using their own words to engage in a relevant, real-life interaction.

PRACTICES A series of substitution drills follows each dialogue. These exercises serve two basic purposes. First, they are designed to reinforce the structure patterns and vocabulary introduced in the dialogue. Second, through substitutions with pertinent topical vocabulary, they are intended to expand the basic concepts of the unit.

PAIR PRACTICE ACTIVITIES A variety of pair practices are used throughout the units. In all cases, it is strongly recommended that the teacher model one sample of the activity several times either with an instructional aide or a student so that all of the students understand what is to be done during the paired activity. Instructors should be sure that students have control of the language required for the activity. The instructor should circulate during the pair practices to monitor progress, keeping in mind that the focus of these activities is on communication. Error correction should be kept to a minimum. The instructor can provide further practice on problem areas with the whole class at a later time.

1. *SUBSTITUTION DIALOGUES* Students practice a dialogue similar to the model dialogue substituting new words or phrases each time. Visuals or words cue the substitutions.

First, the instructor practices the model dialogue using the method described under *Dialogue* in this section of the book. Then the instructor models the first substitution exercise by replacing or substituting the words underlined in the model dialogue with the cued substitutions (usually numbered words in boxes) below the model dialogue.

Example: Model Dialogue
A: How much is the *shirt*?
B: $15.95.
A: Thanks. I'll take it.
First Substitution
A: How much is the blouse?
B: $19.99.
A: Thanks. I'll take it.

| 1. blouse | 1. tie | 1. dress |
| 2. $19.95 | 2. $12.95 | 2. $49.95 |

If the students can handle the first substitution easily, the instructor can have one pair of students demonstrate the next substitution. Then the entire class can practice all of the substitutions in pairs.

2. *CHARTS* Students use cues on grids to ask and answer questions related to an appropriate competency. They enable students to practice with minimal prompts. Chart activities also enable the students to develop the ability to read grids or charts. The following steps are recommended:

a. The instructor models all of the questions and answers on the grid for the whole class, pointing to the appropriate cues on the grid.
b. The instructor asks each question on the grid. Students respond as a whole group.
c. Roles are reversed. The students ask the instructor the questions; the instructor responds.
d. One student is chosen to respond to the "you" section on the chart. The instructor writes in the student's response.
e. Students are paired up for individual pair practice. One pair of students is selected to model several questions and answers for the rest of the class.
f. As the students practice, the instructor circulates to monitor progress and note any structure or pronunciation problems for *later* correction.

As a culminating activity or a review on subsequent days, the instructor can create a blank grid on the board with the same categories and complete the grid with responses from several students.

It is extremely important that the instructor **not** write out the complete questions or answers for the students. Students should use only the minimal cues to generate questions and answers. The purpose of grid activities is for students to practice formulating questions and answers on their own.

INFORMATION GAP ACTIVITIES   The difference between traditional pair practice activities and information gap activities is that in the former, both students have the same information. They are practicing known, predictable questions and responses. In information gap activities, each partner has different information. Students must communicate in order to complete a task. This type of pair practice is obviously more challenging because if the communication is not clear or inadequate, the task cannot be completed. The steps for information gap activities are the same as those for pair practice except that in information gap activities students should not look at each other's papers. Sometimes standing a manila folder between students' materials creates a barrier, or students can sit back to back to minimize the likelihood of students looking at one another's materials. When students realize that they do not have access to their partner's paper, they will be more likely to listen attentively and request clarification to complete the task.

PICTURE SEQUENCES   Several of the units include picture sequences, a series of four visuals designed to progressively illustrate a situation or problem. While the focus of the sequences is the development of oral language skills, they can also be used to practice writing skills.

The picture sequences can be used in various types of activities. The first step in any case is to develop the vocabulary and concepts. As much as possible, this content should be elicited from the students. In some cases, key questions or vocabulary are provided beneath the visuals as cues. Steps to follow may include:

1. Look at each picture in sequence. Elicit and/or provide key vocabulary, identify actions, describe and discuss the situation, answer the question(s) provided.
2. Elicit from students their experiences with similar situations or problems.
3. Have students retell the situation in their own words.
4. Have students in pairs or small groups create dialogues and role play for the whole class.
5. Have students match sentences with visuals and/or put sentence strips in chronological order.
6. Have students write sentences from dictation.
7. Have higher level students write paragraphs, short stories or variations of the situation while the instructor works on oral language skills with the remainder of the class.
8. Relate each situation to students' previous experiences in the U.S. or in their native countries.

INTERVIEWS   Many units in the text include one or more interview activities. These activities are designed to assist students in using previously practiced language and concepts in less controlled situations. Students use the language for the purpose of obtaining real information from their partner(s) and later share this information with the rest of the class.

The first student asks the questions and another responds. The first student listens carefully, asks for repetition or clarification if necessary, and takes notes to assist in sharing the information at the conclusion of the activity. Then roles are reversed and student two asks the questions.

To prepare students for this type of activity, the instructor should first model each question, have students repeat, and check comprehension. If additional preparation is needed, the instructor can ask a student volunteer each question and/or volunteers can ask the instructor the questions. Then pairs or small groups practice while the instructor circulates, provides assistance if needed, and identifies problem areas for total class practice later. The final step is for students to report back, sharing and discussing the information they have obtained. If desired, students' responses may be used to develop a chart or grid for further practice and reenforcement.

READING EXERCISES

1. *READING EXERCISES*   Each unit from 1 to 9 has a narrative reading exercise related to the major topic of the unit. The short, narrative section is followed by two types of comprehension exercises, *WH* questions and Yes/No (True/False) questions.

   Students should read the paragraph silently; then the instructor asks the *WH* questions. Students can be asked to read the part which answers the question, or to tell why they gave a particular answer. They can also be asked to write the answer to the *WH* questions. After circling a Yes or No after each statement, students can be asked to change the "No" (false) statements to "Yes" (true) statements.

   The final section, Write About You, asks the student to provide personal information related to the topic being studied. Instructors can have the students write this information on a separate piece of paper so that they can be gone over and general feedback can be provided.

2. *LIFE SKILLS READINGS*   Where appropriate, reading and writing tasks which the students will encounter outside the classroom have been included. These include numerous types of forms (registration cards, health histories, post office forms, money orders), classified ads, labels, schedules, menus, and pay stubs. Before asking the students to read, interpret, and complete the forms, the instructor should review pertinent vocabulary by asking questions eliciting students' experience related to the task.

HISTORICAL HOLIDAY READINGS (CHAPTER 10)   Activities in this chapter can be introduced as they are celebrated during the school year, or as a separate unit. In either case, the following format is recommended.

1. Use *Holidays*, page 167, to set the scene for discussions about holidays in general. These activities should generate a general discussion of the concept of "holiday" or special day in all countries. From this general discussion, an overview of the American holidays to be studied will follow. Use the small calendars on the page as well as larger school calendars. Special emphasis can be placed on universal celebrations.

2. *Before You Read* activities are intended to develop a context for and the vocabulary needed to comprehend the reading. First, the teacher should discuss the new vocabulary, asking if students know the meaning of the words. If no one knows the word, provide meaning by visuals, examples, demonstration. Next try to determine if a similar holiday is celebrated in students' countries. Next, ask students the questions provided under the *Talk with Your Teacher* section. Write their responses on the board. Do not provide the correct answers. Tell the students that the accuracy of these answers will be verified after the reading.

3. *HOLIDAY READINGS (MARTIN LUTHER KING DAY*, ETC.) Ideally, the students should read each paragraph silently, by themselves, in order to answer the questions. If this is not possible, for the first reading, the instructor can read as the students follow along and listen before reading silently and then answering the questions.

4. On the day after the holiday, the instructor can discuss with the students what they experienced related to the holiday. Did they see any signs related to the holiday? Did they read, hear or see any news or programs related to the holiday? Did they celebrate the holiday with an American neighbor or friend? A re-reading of the narrative may also be appropriate.

5. After discussing important holidays celebrated in the students' countries, the instructor can write and have duplicated a short narrative reading. The instructor, and/or the students, can formulate Yes/No and WH questions to be answered following the silent reading.

chapter 1

IDENTIFICATION AND COMMUNICATION

COMPETENCY OBJECTIVES

On completion of this chapter, the students will show orally, in writing, or through demonstration that they are able to use language needed in the following situations:

A. PERSONAL INFORMATION AND INTRODUCTIONS

- Give, on request, self-identification and personal information, including name, address, telephone number, nationality, education, marital status, and occupation.
- Fill out simple forms.
- Identify teacher's name.
- Make and respond to simple greetings and introductions.

B. STATES OF BEING AND FEELINGS

- Express feelings and states of being.

C. FAMILY RELATIONSHIPS

- Identify members of immediate and extended family.

D. TELLING TIME

- Tell time in minutes and hours.
- Identify periods of time in days, months, and years.

E. TELEPHONE COMMUNICATION

- Answer incoming calls.
- Take simple messages.

HOW ARE YOU?

A: Hello. How are you?
B: Fine, thank you. And you?
A: Just fine, thanks.

PRACTICE

Hello.   How are you?
Good morning.
Good afternoon.
Good evening.

Fine,   thank you.
Just fine,   thanks.
Not too bad,
So so,

I'M HAPPY TO MEET YOU.

A: Bill, this is Tom.
B: I'm happy to meet you, Tom.
A: Thank you. The same to you.

PRACTICE

Bill, this is Tom.
        my wife.
        my husband.
        my teacher, Mr. _____ .

        My principal, Mrs. _____ .

I'm happy to meet you.
    glad
    pleased

Pair Practice: Introduce your partner to two other students.

Do they shake hands?
Do people shake hands in your country?

WHAT'S YOUR NAME?

A: Hello. Let's fill out your registration card.
   What's your name?
B: My name is Joe Brown.
A: What's your address?
B: 1632 Broadway Street.
A: And your zip code?
B: 92102.

MY NAME IS...

PRACTICE

What's your name?
   his   first name?
   her   last name?
   their family name?
   your middle name?

What's your address?
          telephone number?
          Social Security number?

1 - one	6 - six
2 - two	7 - seven
3 - three	8 - eight
4 - four	9 - nine
5 - five	10 - ten

What's your zip code?
   their
   his/her

1 **Miss Helen Park**
   734 Oak Street
   Austin, TX
                    78768

2 **Mr. Joe Brown**
   1130 Olympia Way
   San Francisco, CA
                    94131

3 **Mrs. Mary King**
   195 Congress Street
   Brooklyn, NY
                    11201

4 **Mr. & Mrs. Tom Luna**
   613 West Avenue
   Los Angeles, CA
                    91365

INTERVIEW

Look at the addresses in the boxes above. Then ask and answer these questions with your teacher.

1. Who lives in Austin?
2. Who lives on Congress Street?
3. Where do Mr. and Mrs. Luna live?
4. What street does Joe Brown live on?

Fill in the forms. Use the information from the forms on page 3 to fill in these forms. Do the first one with your teacher.

1

Name Park, _____
        Last   First

Address 734 _____
         #   Street

           TX _____
City   State   Zip code

2

Name _____ Joe _____
        Last   First

Address _____ Olympia Way
         #   Street

San Francisco _____
City   State   Zip code

3

Name _____
        Last   First

Address 195 _____
         #   Street

                      11201
City   State   Zip code

4

Name _____
        Last   First

Address _____
         #   Street

_____
City   State   Zip code

Fill in this form with information about yourself.

ADULT SCHOOL REGISTRATION

Name _____
        Last   First

Address _____
        #   Street

_____
City   State   Zip code

Talk about the following pictures with your teacher, your class, and then with your partner. Answer the questions about each picture.

1. Where are the students?
   What do they say?

2. Who do they see?
   What does he say?

3. The young man introduces his friend.
   What does the principal say?

4. The friends meet in the hall.
   What do they say?

INTERVIEW

What do you say when you see a friend? a teacher?
What do you say when you meet a new friend?

WHERE ARE YOU FROM?

A: Hi. I'm from Japan.
Where are you from?
B: I'm from Mexico.
A: Are you a student here?
B: Yes, my teacher is Mrs. Scott.

PRACTICE

I am	from Mexico.	I'm	from	Japan.
You are		You're		Mexico.
He/She/It is		He's		California.
We are		She's		Florida.
You are		We're		Korea.
They are		They're		Iran.

Are you	from Mexico?
Is he/she/it	
Are we	
Are you	
Are they	

Where are you from?
Where were you born?
What is your birthplace?
What is your country of birth?

Name	Country	Student	Teacher
Tam	Vietnam	Yes	Mrs. Brown
Ali	Iran	Yes	Mr. Smith
Maria	Mexico	Yes	Ms. Lee
You	?	?	?

Pair Practice: Ask and answer the following questions with your teacher. Then, ask your partner about Tam, Ali, and Maria. Then tell about yourself.

EXAMPLE:
1. Where is Tam from?   Vietnam.
2. Is he a student?   Yes, he is.
3. Who is his teacher?   Mrs. Brown.

YOUR JOB

A: What is your occupation?
B: What?
A: What is your job?
B: What?
A: What do you *do*?
B: Oh, I go to school. I'm a student.

PRACTICE

What is your occupation?   What kind of job do you have?
               job?   What kind of work   do?
               work?

I'm a student.   I'm unemployed.
      homemaker.   retired.
      mechanic.   out of work.

Pair Practice: Practice the following conversations with your teacher. Then practice with your partner.

A: What's your occupation?
B: I'm a <u>secretary</u>.
           1
A: <u>What</u>?
   2
B: I'm a <u>secretary</u>.
           1

| 1. nurse | 1. mechanic | 1. student | 1. ? |
| 2. Excuse me? | 2. Pardon me? | 2. Huh? | 2. ? |

Tell about yourself.

EXAMPLE: A: What's your occupation?
             B: I'm a <u>nurse</u>.
                    1
             A: <u>Excuse me</u>?
                  2
             B: I'm a <u>nurse</u>.
                    1

1

_____

2

_____

3

_____

4

_____

5

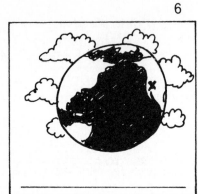

_____

6

_____

7

_____

8

_____

9

_____

Ask and answer a question about each picture with your teacher. Then ask your partner the questions.

EXAMPLE: 1. What is your name?   My name is _____ .

2. What is your address?   My address is _____ .

Fill in Form 1 with information about yourself.

1 | Name _____ ☐ married
☐ single

Address _____

Telephone ( ) _____ Social Security number ___ - ___ - ___

Country of birth _____ Birthdate _____

Occupation _____

Fill in Form 2 with information about your partner. Ask your partner how to spell words that you do not know.

2 | Name _____ ☐ married
☐ single

Address _____

Telephone ( ) _____ Social Security number ___ - ___ - ___

Country of birth _____ Birthdate _____

Occupation _____

HOW ARE YOU?

A: How are you tonight?
B: Tired, how about you?
A: I'm not tired, but I'm sleepy.

PRACTICE

I'm tired.	How about you?	I'm *not* tired.
sleepy.		You're *not* sleepy.
hungry.		He's/She's *not* hungry.
thirsty.		We're *not* thirsty.
busy.		You're *not* busy.
happy.		They're *not* happy.

Pair Practice: Ask and answer questions with your teacher and then with your partner. Use the example as a model. Ask about John, Pedro, Saeed, Katy and your partner.

	HOT	HUNGRY	ANGRY	SLEEPY
John	Yes	Yes	No	No
Pedro	No	No	Yes	No
Saeed	No	Yes	No	Yes
Katy	Yes	No	Yes	No
You	?	?	?	?

EXAMPLE: Is John hot? Yes, he is.
Is John hungry? Yes, he is.
Is John angry? No, he's not.
Is John sleepy? No, he's not.

Pair Practice: Ask and answer a question about each picture with your teacher. Then ask your partner the questions.

EXAMPLE: Is he hot? Yes, he is.

Group Activity: Find pictures in magazines that show the following feelings. Tell your group about the pictures.

hot	angry	happy
sleepy	hungry	sad
sick	thirsty	bored

YOUR FAMILY

A: Are you married?
B: Yes, I am.
A: Tell me about your family.
   How many children do
   you have?
B: I have two children, one son
   and one daughter.

PRACTICE

Tell me about your family.
                husband.
                wife.
                children.

one child	-	two children
one man	-	two men
one woman	-	two women

How many children do you   have?
                does he
                does she
                do they

I have two children.
He has one child.
She has four children
They have three children.

Are you married? Yes, I am.
                No, I'm not. I'm single.
                            divorced.
                            a widow.

I don't have   any children.
He doesn't
She doesn't
They don't

Pair Practice: Ask your partner about his or her family.

HOW OLD ARE YOUR CHILDREN?

A: How old are your children?
B: My son is 16 years old.
   My daughter is 10.
A: Are they in school?
B: Yes. He's a junior in high school.
   She's in elementary school.

PRACTICE

How old is your daughter?
              son?
How old are your children?
              his
              her
              their
She's in preschool.
         elementary school.
         middle school.
         junior high school.
         senior high school.
         college.

Pair Practice: Ask your partner if he or she has children. Then ask about the children's schools.

Pair Practice: Ask and answer questions about this family with your teacher. Then ask your partner the questions.

Example: Where is the grandmother? aunt? brother-in-law?

Tell about your family.

DESCRIBE YOUR FAMILY

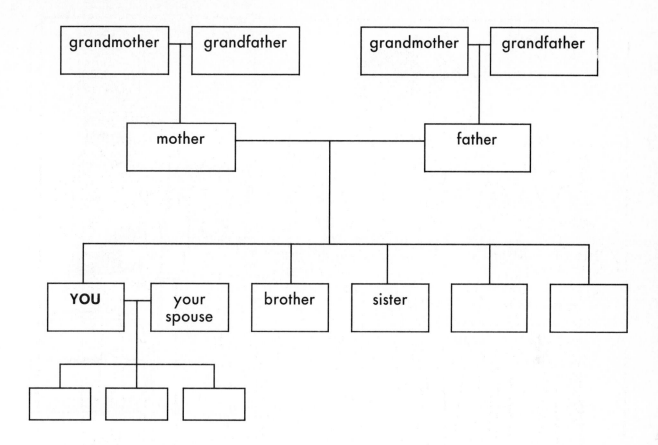

Fill in the boxes with the names of people in your family. Tell the class about your family.

INTERVIEW

Ask and answer these questions with your teacher and then with your partner.

1. Are you married?
2. Do you have any children?
   How old are they?
   What are they doing now?
3. Do you have any brothers or sisters?
   Where do they live?
   What are they doing now?
4. Are your mother and father living?
   Where do they live?
5. Do you have any relatives in the United States? Who are they?
   Where do they live?
6. Do you have any grandchildren?

WHAT TIME IS IT?

A: What time is it?
B: I think it's 7 o'clock.
A: Let's turn on the TV.
It's time for the news.
B: OK.

PRACTICE

It is 7 o'clock.　　　　　　seven
　　8　　　　　　　　　　　eight
　　5　　　　　　　　　　　five
　　8:30 A.M.　　　　　　eight-thirty
　　6:15 P.M.　　　　　　six-fifteen

It is time for the news.
　　　　　　school.
　　　　　　coffee.
　　　　　　a break.

It's 6 o'clock.

My watch is slow.

My watch is fast.

My watch is broken.

WHAT'S THE DATE?

A: What day is it?
B: It's Wednesday.
A: What's the date?
B: It's April 14, 19 ____ .

PRACTICE

It's Monday.
   Tuesday.
   Wednesday.
   Thursday.
   Friday.
   Saturday.
   Sunday.

It's January.
   February.
   March.
   April.
   May.
   June.
   July.
   August.
   September.
   October.
   November.
   December.

It's the first.
   second.
   third.
   fourth.
   fifth.
   sixth.
   seventh.
   eighth.
   ninth.
   tenth.
   eleventh.
   twelfth.
   thirteenth.
   twentieth.

When's the party?
   Christmas?
   your birthday?
   our vacation?

Pair Practice: Ask your partner these questions.

What days do you come to school?
What days do you go to work?
When is your birthday?
When do you go on vacation?

Group Practice: Line up around the room in order of your birthday month. Call out your birthday month to make sure you are in the right order.

WHEN DO YOU GO TO SCHOOL? _____

A: When do you go to school?
B: Five days a week. How about you?
A: I usually go three times a week.

PRACTICE

I always go to school.
  usually
  sometimes
  never

When do you go to school?
How often   watch TV?
             work?

I go to school once a week.
             twice a week.
             three times a week.

Pair Practice: Ask and answer questions about Su, Anh, Jose, Maria and your partner with your teacher and then with your partner.

Use these words in your answers: *always, usually, sometimes, never.*

Example: How often does Su go to school? Su always goes to school.

SCHOOL ATTENDANCE					
	M	T	W	TH	F
Su	✔	✔	✔	✔	✔
Anh	✔		✔	✔	
Jose	✔	✔	✔	✔	
Maria					
Partner	?	?	?	?	?

Pair Practice: Ask and answer a question about each picture with your teacher. Then ask your partner the questions.

Example: How often do you go to school? I go to school twice a week.

HELLO, IT'S FOR YOU

A: Hello.
B: Hello. This is Bill. Is Tom there?
A: Yes. Just a minute, please.
   Tom, it's for you.

PRACTICE

Just a minute, please.
    moment
    second

Tom, it's for you.
    telephone.

IS SUE THERE?

A: Hello.
B: Hello. Is Sue there?
A: No, she's not. May I take a message?
B: Yes. This is Tom. Please tell her I'll call later.
A: All right, I will. Good-bye.

PRACTICE

Tell her I'll call later.
         tomorrow.
         next week.
         back.

May I take a message?
Can

I'll call her next week.
You'll
He'll
She'll
They'll

INTERVIEW

1. Do you have a telephone?
2. Do you speak in English or in your native language?
3. Do your children use the phone?

PHONE MESSAGES

Pair Practice: Practice the following conversations with your teacher and then with a partner.

A: Hello, is <u>Sam</u> there?
         1
B: Yes, <u>he</u> is. Just a <u>moment</u>, please.
          2   3

Phone Memo

Mrs. Brown —

Carl called

1. Sally	1. Bill	1. Ann
2. she	2. he	2. she
3. minute	3. second	3. moment

EXAMPLE: A: Hello, is <u>Sally</u> there?
                    B: Yes, <u>she</u> is. Just a <u>minute</u>, please.

A: Hello. Is <u>Susan</u> there?
                       1
B: No, <u>she's</u> not. Can I take a
              2
message?
A: Yes. Please tell <u>her</u> <u>Bill</u> called.
                                3   4

Phone Memo

Anne —

Bob called

1. Mary	1. Bob	1. Mr. Green	1. Mrs. Brown
2. she's	2. he's	2. ?	2. ?
3. her	3. him	3. ?	3. ?
4. Tom	4. Ann	4. John	4. Carl

EXAMPLE: A: Hello. Is <u>Mary</u> there?
                    B: No, <u>she's</u> not. Can I take a message?
                    A: Yes. Please tell <u>her</u> <u>Tom</u> called.

READING EXERCISE

Jose goes to school to study English. He usually goes four days a week. Jose is not married; he is single. He lives with his sister. His sister is married and has two children.

QUESTIONS

1. Does Jose go to school?
2. What does he study?
3. Who does he live with?

YES/NO

Read each sentence. Circle yes or no after each sentence.

1. Jose goes to school to study Spanish.   Yes   (No)
2. Jose is single.   Yes   No
3. Jose lives with his brother.   Yes   No

WRITE ABOUT YOURSELF

1. My name is _____ .

2. I am from _____ .

3. My address is _____ .

4. My zip code is _____ .

5. I come to school to study _____ .

6. I am a _____ .

chapter 2

FOOD

COMPETENCY OBJECTIVES

On completion of this chapter the students will show orally, in writing, or through demonstration that they are able to use language needed in the following situations:

A. SHOPPING FOR FOOD

- Identify and name the most common foods.
- Ask for and locate foods in a market.
- Compare stores and prices.
- Differentiate between types of stores—supermarket, discount, and 24-hour.

B. EATING OUT

- Order at a fast-food restaurant.
- Refuse offers of food.

C. CHANGE AND MONEY

- Ask for and make change.

LET'S GO TO THE STORE

A: We need to go to the store.
B: OK. I need a lot of things.
A: Do you want to go to 7-Eleven, Safeway, or Fed-Mart?
B: Let's go to Fed-Mart. It's the cheapest.

1. 24-hour   2. Discount   3. Supermarket

PRACTICE

We need to go to the store.
         market.
         bakery.

We need a lot of things.
     many
     several
     a few
     a couple

Let's go to Safeway.
         Fed-Mart.
         7-Eleven.

Let's go to the store.
         supermarket.
         bakery.

Milk is cheap at 7-Eleven.
Milk is cheaper at Safeway.
Milk is cheapest at Fed-Mart.

Pair Practice: Ask and answer these questions with your teacher. Then ask your partner.

Example: A. What is a 24-hour store?
           B: It is open day and night. It doesn't close.

1. What is a discount store?
2. What is a supermarket?
3. What store do you go to?
4. How often do you go to the store?

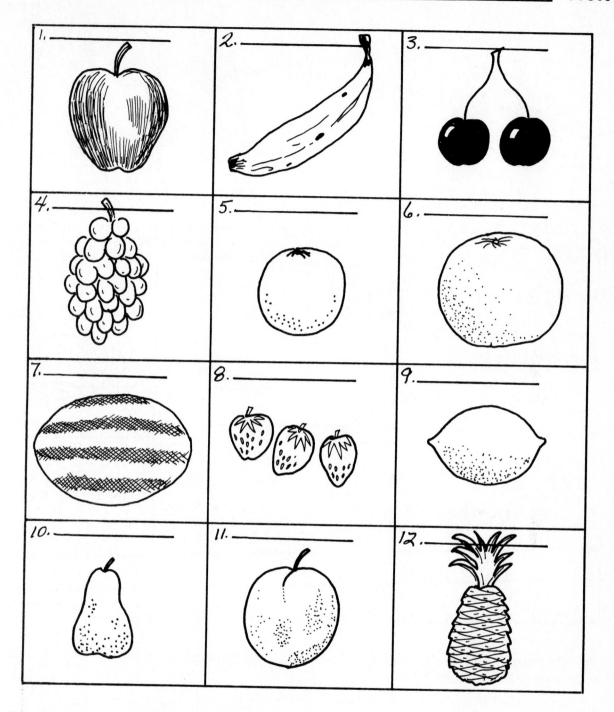

Pair Practice: Ask and answer questions about the fruit with your teacher and then with your partner.

EXAMPLE: **1.** Do you want an apple? Yes, I do./No, I don't.
            2. Do you buy bananas?

apple	cherries	lemon	grapefruit
watermelon	strawberries	orange	peach
banana	grapes	pear	pineapple

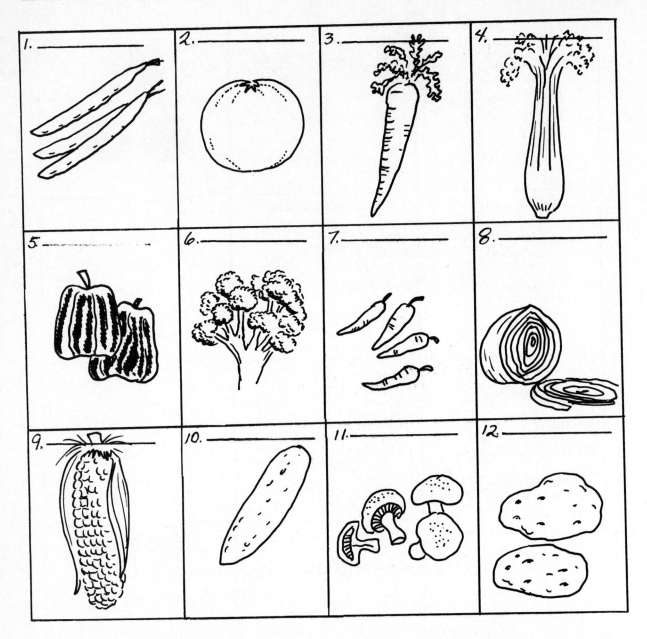

1. _____
2. _____
3. _____
4. _____
5. _____
6. _____
7. _____
8. _____
9. _____
10. _____
11. _____
12. _____

Pair Practice: Ask and answer questions about the vegetables with your teacher and then with your partner.

EXAMPLE: **1.**   Do you eat green beans?   Yes, I do./No, I don't.
                  2.   Do you want a tomato?

green beans	carrot	celery	pepper
chili	onions/green onion	cucumber	broccoli
tomato	corn	mushrooms	potato

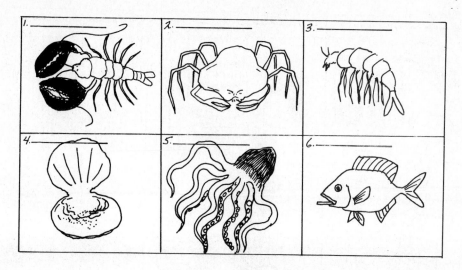

Pair Practice: Ask and answer questions about each picture with your teacher and then with your partner.

EXAMPLE: **1.**   Do you eat lobster   Yes, I do./No, I don't.
            2.   Where can you get lobster?

lobster   crab   shrimp   clam   octopus   fish

Meat/Poultry

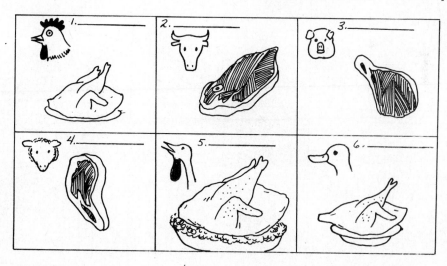

Pair Practice: Ask and answer questions about each picture with your teacher and then with your partner.

EXAMPLE: **1.**   Do you like chicken?   Yes, I do./No, I don't.
            2.   Do you buy beef?

chicken   beef   pork   lamb   turkey   duck

1. _____
2. _____
3. _____
4. _____
5. _____
6. _____
7. _____
8. _____
9. _____
10. _____
11. _____
12. _____

Pair Practice: Ask and answer questions about each picture with your teacher and then with your partner.

EXAMPLE:
1. Do you need a box of cereal? Yes, I do./No, I don't.
2. What do you buy that is in a box?

box	bottle	carton	bunch
cube	package	six-pack	bag
can	loaf	jar	head

WHAT DO WE NEED?

A: What do we need at the store?
B: We need a carton of milk, a pound of bacon, and a loaf of bread.
A: Do we need eggs?
B: Yes. Please get a dozen.

PRACTICE

We need a carton of . . . .
    box
    loaf
    stick/cube
    can
    bottle
    jar
    bag
    package
    bunch
    six-pack

We need a quart of . . . .
    pound
    gallon

Pair Practice: Ask and answer these questions with your teacher. Then ask your partner.

1. What do you buy in a carton?
2. What do you buy in a bottle?
3. What do you buy in a bunch?
4. What do you buy in a six-pack?

Pair Practice: Ask and answer questions about the food in the refrigerator with your teacher and then with your partner.

EXAMPLE: 1. How much milk do we have? One-half gallon.
          2. How many onions do we have? Three.

BUYING FISH

A. How much is the fish?
B: It's $2.79 a pound. Do you want this one?
   It weighs 3 pounds.
A: Yes, I'll take it.
B: Is that all?
A: Yes, that's all today.

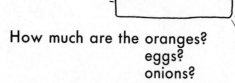

PRACTICE

How much is the fish?
      coffee?
      pork?

How much does the fish cost?
      coffee
      pork

What is the price of the fish?
      oranges?
      coffee?
      eggs?

How much are the oranges?
      eggs?
      onions?

How much do the oranges cost?
      eggs
      onions

Pair Practice: Ask and answer these questions with your teacher. Then ask your partner.

1. Do you like fish?
2. Do you eat fish?
3. How often do you eat fish?
4. Where do you buy fish?

SUPER SALE!

AT THE GOLDEN CARROT SUPERMART

EXTRA LEAN GROUND BEEF $2.39 lb.

GOLDEN DELICIOUS APPLES .69 lb

AVOCADOS ----- .89 ea.
PEARS ------ .59 lb
LETTUCE ------ .69 ea.
STRAWBERRIES -- .99 basket

SMILE TOOTHPASTE --- 1.67
FAMILY'S COOKIES ---- .89
SUN ORANGE JUICE -- .72

LARGE GRADE A EGGS 1 DOZEN $1.29

STORE HOURS:
MON - FRI.
10 to 9 PM
SAT & SUN
10 to 6

USDA GRADE A FRYER FRESH & PAN-READY .69 lb.

Pair Practice: Ask and answer questions about the prices of the items in the ad with your teacher and your class. Use the example as a model.

EXAMPLE: How much is the lettuce?
How much are the eggs?

The Grocery Store

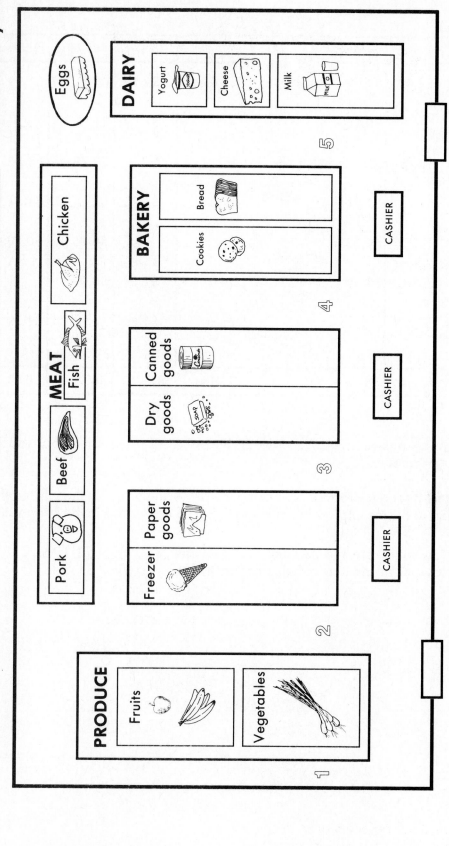

PRODUCE
Fruits
Vegetables

1

MEAT
Pork   Beef   Fish   Chicken

Freezer   Paper goods   Dry goods   Canned goods

BAKERY
Cookies   Bread

DAIRY
Eggs
Yogurt   Cheese   Milk

CASHIER   CASHIER   CASHIER   CASHIER

2   3   4   5

Pair Practice: Ask and answer questions about the grocery store with your teacher and then with your partner. Use the example as a model.

EXAMPLE: Where's the bread?
It's in the bakery section, aisle 5.

| bread | apples | soap | ice cream | cookies | milk | pork | soup |
| chicken | yogurt | bananas | cheese | napkins | lettuce | fish | cashier |

A

	7-Eleven	Fed-Mart	Safeway
cookies	$2.19	$1.89	$1.99
milk	$1.99	_____	$0.98
soap	$0.85	$0.78	_____
bread	_____	$1.33	$1.54
bananas	$0.55 lb.	_____	$0.33 lb.
soda	_____	$0.99	$1.49
eggs	$1.89	$1.59	_____
TOTAL	$11.46	$8.10	$8.94

B

	7-Eleven	Fed-Mart	Safeway
cookies	$2.19	$1.89	$1.99
milk	$1.99	$1.27	_____
soap	_____	$0.78	$0.82
bread	$1.70	_____	$1.54
bananas	_____	$0.25 lb.	$0.33 lb.
soda	$2.29	$0.99	_____
eggs	$1.89	_____	$1.79
TOTAL	$11.46	$6.10	$8.94

Pair Practice: Ask and answer questions about the prices of items with your teacher and then with your partner.

Student A asks Student B for the information missing in Part A and writes in the information. Student B asks Student A for the information missing in Part B and writes in the information.

EXAMPLE: A: How much are the cookies at 7-Eleven?   B: $2.19.
            B: How much are the cookies at Fed-Mart?   A: $1.89.

WHERE'S THE MILK?

A: Excuse me. Where's the milk?
B: It's in the dairy section, in aisle 3.
A: Where?
B: Dairy section, aisle 3.
A: Thank you.

PRACTICE

Where's the milk?
       lettuce?
       bread?
       meat?
       cashier?
       checkout?
       exit?

It's in the dairy section.
       produce
       bakery
       meat department.
       dry goods

Where are the eggs?
       vegetables and fruit?
       paper towels?
       frozen foods?
       cookies?

It's at the front of the store.
    in   back

They're in the dairy section.
       produce
       paper goods
       freezer
       bakery

Pair Practice: Ask and answer these questions with your teacher. Then ask your partner.

1. Where do you shop for food?
2. Is it a supermarket or a small store?
3. Do you ask for help?

THIS MILK IS SOUR

A: May I speak to the manager?
B: I'm the manager. Can I help you?
A: Yes. I want to return this milk. It's sour.
B: You're right. It's past the expiration date.
   I'll get you a fresh carton.

PRACTICE

I want to return this milk.
    bread.
    meat.
    fruit.
    cereal.
    flour.
    fish.
    shrimp.

It's sour.
  moldy.
  old.
  rotten.
It has bugs.
   worms.
It smells.

Pair Practice: Ask and answer these questions with your teacher. Then ask your partner.

1. What is the expiration date on the gallon of milk?
2. Did you ever buy food that had bugs?
3. What did you do? Did you throw it away?
4. Did you go back to that store?
5. Do you need a receipt to return food?
6. What can you do if you don't have a receipt and you need to return food?

Pair Practice: Ask and answer these questions with your teacher. Then ask your partner.

1. What is the expiration date on the milk?
2. What is the expiration date on the corn?
3. What is the expiration date on the chicken?
4. What is the matter with the bread?
5. What is wrong with the apples?
6. What is the problem with the cereal?
7. What is the expiration date on the yogurt?

ORDERING FAST FOOD

A: Can I help you?
B: Yes. I'd like a hamburger and French fries.
A: Anything to drink?
B: A large Coke.
A: Anything else?
B: No thanks.

PRACTICE

Can I help you?
    take your order?
Are you ready to order?
Would you like   ?

Yes, I'd like a hot dog.
    hamburger.
    large Coke.
    medium
    small

Pair Practice: Ask and answer these questions with your teacher. Then ask your partner.

1. What is fast food?
2. What kinds of fast-food restaurants are there?
3. Do you go to fast-food restaurants?
4. What is your favorite fast-food restaurant?
5. What do you usually order?
6. Do you have fast food in your country?
    What kinds?

GET & GO FAST FOOD

	Hamburgers	$1.79
	Cheeseburgers	$1.99
	Fish Sandwich	$2.29
	Chicken Sandwich	$2.49
	Hot Dog	$ .99
	French Fries	$ .89
	Onion Rings	$1.09
	Salad	$1.75
	Small Drink	$ .65
	Medium Drink	$ .80
	Large Drink	$1.00
	Coffee, Tea	$ .50
	Cookies (each)	$ .75

Pair Practice: Ask and answer these questions with your teacher. Then ask your partner.

1. How much is a hamburger?
2. How much is a cheeseburger?
3. How much is an order of French fries?
4. How much is a small orange drink?
5. How much is a cookie?
6. How much is coffee?
7. How much is a fish sandwich?
8. How much is a salad?
9. How much is a chicken sandwich?
10. How much is an order of onion rings?

MAKING CHANGE

A: Excuse me, do you have change for a dollar?
B: Yes, I do. Here you are—50, 75, 85, 95, a dollar.
A: Thank you. I want to buy a soda.
B: Use this machine. That one is out of order.

A: Excuse me, do you have change for a dollar?
B: No, I don't. I'm sorry.
A: Thank you anyway.

PRACTICE

Do you have change for a quarter?
       dollar?
              5 dollars?
              20 dollars?

That one is out of order.
         not working.
         broken.

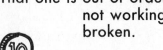

I want to buy a soda.
           soft drink.
coffee.
tea.

Pair Practice: Ask your partner these questions.

1. Does your school have food or drink machines?
2. Where are they?
3. What foods or drinks are in the machines?
4. What foods or drinks do you buy from the machines?
5. What do you do if you don't have change?

REFUSING OFFERS OF FOOD

A: Aren't potlucks fun?
    There are so many different foods.
B: Yes. Everything is delicious.
A: Try a shrimp roll. Here, have one.
B: Oh, no thank you.
    I don't care for shrimp.

PRACTICE

Here, have one.
    try

Try some.
Have

Would you like some?
    care for some shrimp?

No, thanks. But thank you anyway.
I don't care for any now.

No, thank you. I don't like shrimp.
    I don't care for shrimp.
    I can't eat shrimp.
    I'm allergic to shrimp.

Pair Practice: Ask and answer these questions with your teacher. Then ask your partner.

1. What foods do you like?
2. What foods don't you like?
3. Are you allergic to any foods? Which ones?
4. What are your favorite American foods?
5. What American foods don't you like?
6. What kinds of food do you eat in your country?

Every week, Mrs. Lew goes to the supermarket. She buys a lot of things. She always buys a quart of milk, a dozen eggs, and a loaf of bread. Sometimes she needs a pound of coffee. If she doesn't have any flour or sugar, she buys them. She goes to the bakery section for bread. She goes to the dairy section for milk and butter. She goes to the produce section for lettuce and tomatoes.

QUESTIONS

1. Where does Mrs. Lew go every week?
2. What does she always buy?
3. What section is the bread in?
4. What section are the lettuce and tomatoes in?

YES/NO

Read each sentence. Circle yes or no after each sentence.

1. She buys a lot of things.   (Yes) No
2. She always buys a jar of milk.   Yes   No
3. She always buys eggs.   Yes   No
4. She always buys a loaf of bread.   Yes   No
5. She goes to the bakery section for beef.   Yes   No
6. She goes to the produce section for lettuce and bread.   Yes   No

WRITE ABOUT YOURSELF

1. Do you go to the supermarket every week? _____

   _____

2. Which store do you go to? _____

   _____

3. What do you always buy? _____

   _____

4. Do you buy milk, eggs, and coffee? _____

   _____

chapter 3

HEALTH

COMPETENCY OBJECTIVES

On completion of this chapter the students will show orally, in writing, or through demonstration that they are able to use language needed in the following situations.

A. PARTS OF THE BODY

- Identify major external and internal parts of the body.
- Describe and state common health problems.
- Express sympathy.

B. APPOINTMENTS

- Make appointments.
- Fill out a simple health information form.
- Ask for clarification.

C. PRESCRIPTION AND NONPRESCRIPTION MEDICINE

- Identify dosages of medicines.
- Follow oral or written directions for taking medications.
- Ask for nonprescription medicine

D. EMERGENCY SITUATIONS

- Respond to health emergencies by caling 911, police, poison control, hospital, or other resources.
- Describe emergency situations.
- Use the telephone to give personal information and report the location of an emergency.

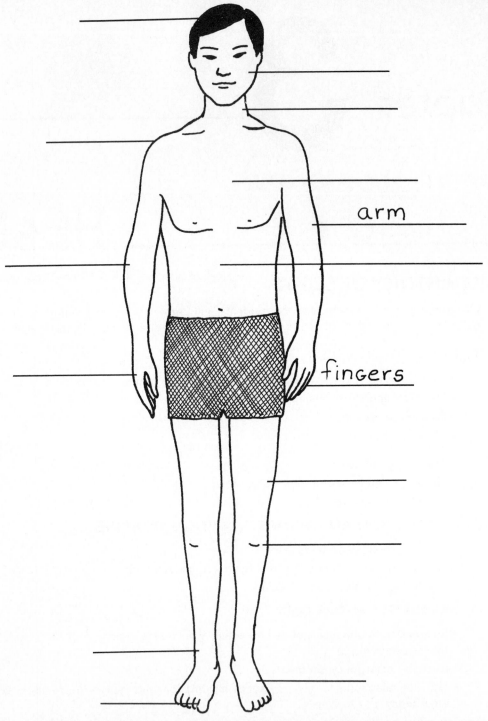

arm

fingers

Pair Practice: Talk about the parts of the body with your teacher and then with your partner. Then write the name of the part on the correct line. Use the example as a model.

EXAMPLE: My arm hurts
My fingers hurt.

head	neck	shoulder	ankle	elbow
hand	fingers	knee	arm	toes
face	leg	chest	foot	stomach

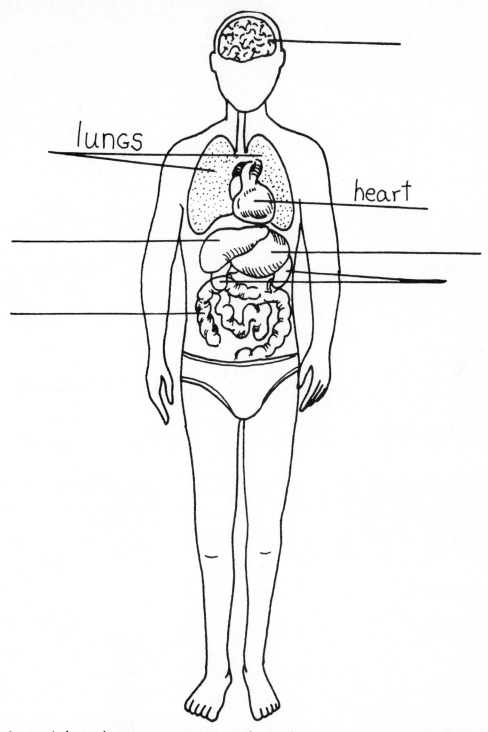

lungs

heart

Pair Practice: Ask and answer questions about the parts inside the body with your teacher and then with your partner. Then write the name of the part on the correct line. Use the example as a model.

EXAMPLE: Where is the heart?
           Where are the lungs?

brain   lungs   heart   liver   stomach   kidneys   intestines

WHAT'S THE MATTER?

A: What's the matter?
B: I have a headache.
A: Oh, I'm so sorry.
B: Thanks. I'll be OK.

PRACTICE

What's the matter?
         problem?
      wrong?

What happened?

I'm so sorry.
   sorry.
   sorry to hear that.

I have a headache.
She has toothache.
He   an earache.

I'll be OK.
    fine.
    better.
    all right.

MY ANKLE HURTS

A: What's wrong?
B: My ankle hurts.
A: That's too bad.
    What did you do?
B: I sprained it yesterday.

PRACTICE

My ankle hurts.
   back
   arm

What did you do?
     happened?

What's wrong?

I sprained it yesterday.
   cut   this morning.
   broke   last night.

Pair Practice: Ask and answer questions about each picture with your teacher. Then ask your partner.

EXAMPLE: A: What's the matter?
B: I have a stomachache.
an earache.

stomachache   toothache   headache   earache   backache   _____ ?

47

Pair Practice: Ask and answer questions about each picture with your teacher. Then ask your partner.

EXAMPLE: A: What's wrong?
B: My shoulder hurts.

shoulder   leg   elbow   hand   foot   throat

WHERE WERE YOU YESTERDAY?

A: Where were you yesterday?
We missed you.
B: I was sick and stayed home.
My kids were sick, too.
A: I'm sorry to hear that.
B: Thanks, but we're better today.

PRACTICE

Where were you yesterday?
              they
    was he/she
              Tom

I'm fine.
She's OK.
He's better.
They're all right.

I was sick.
       home.
       at the clinic.
       at the doctor's office.

Pair Practice: Ask and answer questions with your teacher and then with your partner. Use the example as a model. Ask about Tom, Toan, Gloria, and your partner. Fill in the chart with information about your partner.

WHERE WERE YOU?				
NAME	WHERE?	WHEN?	WHY?	HOW IS/ARE _____ TODAY?
Tom	home	yesterday	sick	OK
Toan	doctor	this morning	sore throat	better
Gloria	school	last Friday	talk to teacher	fine
You	?	?	?	?

EXAMPLE:
1. Where was Tom yesterday?   At home.
2. When was Tom at home?   Yesterday.
3. Why was Tom at home?   He was sick.
4. How is Tom today?   He's OK.

Nov. 29, 1990

Dear Mrs. Wong:

Please excuse Juan. He was absent yesterday. He had a stomachache. He's fine today. Thank you.

Mrs. Salazar

QUESTIONS

1. Who was absent?
2. When as he absent?
3. Why was he absent?
4. How is he today?

YES/NO

Read each sentence. Circle yes or no after each sentence.

1. The teacher's name is Mrs. Salazar.   Yes   (No)
2. Juan was absent yesterday.   Yes   No
3. Mrs. Salazar had a stomachache.   Yes   No
4. Juan is fine today.   Yes   No

WRITE ABOUT YOURSELF

1. How were you yesterday? _____

2. How are you today? _____

Pair Practice: Ask and answer questions with your teacher and then with your partner. Use the example as a model.

TEACHER	STUDENT	WHY
Miss Yang	Donna	went to the dentist
Mr. Black	Joe	had the flu
_____ (your teacher)	_____ (your partner)	_____

EXAMPLE: 1. Who is the teacher?   Miss Yang.
          2. Who is the student?   Donna.
          3. Why was Donna absent?   She went to the dentist.

Use the information about your partner on the chart to write a letter to the teacher excusing your partner's absence.

Use the letter on page 50 to help you write your letter.

```
                                    _____

_____ :

_____

_____

_____

_____

                            _____
```

HOW DO YOU FEEL?

A: How do you feel?
B: Not so good. My ear aches.
   I have a fever, too.
   My temperature is 101°.
A: You should go to the doctor.
B: You're right.
   I'll call the doctor's office now.

PRACTICE

How do you feel?
How are you?
Not so good.
Awful.
Pretty bad.

You should go to the doctor.
          call the dentist.
          see

Reading the Thermometer

1. What is this temperature? _____

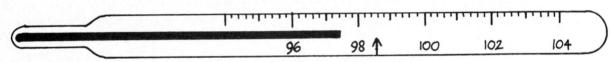

2. What is this temperature? _____

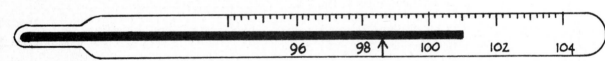

3. Show a *normal* adult temperature on the thermometer.

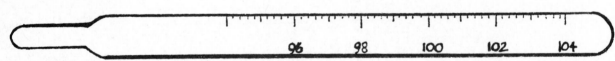

Pair Practice: Ask and answer questions about the thermometer with your teacher. Then ask your partner.

EXAMPLE: 1. Do you use a thermometer?
         2. Are the thermometers the same in the U.S. as in your country?

MAKING AN APPOINTMENT

A: Dr. Lam's office.
   May I help you?
B: Yes, this is Bob Coleman.
   I need to see the dentist.
A: What's the matter, Bob?
B: My tooth aches a lot.
A: We can see you at 4:30.
   Can you come in then?
B: Yes, I can. Thanks a lot.

PRACTICE

I need to see the dentist.
  want
  have   make an appointment.

We can see you.
  take

Dr. G. R. Lam

Name _Bob Coleman_

Next Appt. _Tues 6/18_

Time _9:00_ A.M.

Joseph Olivos, DDS

Name _Mary Loo_

Appointment _Fri. April 16_

Time _2:30_ P.M.

Pair Practice: Ask and answer questions about Bob's and Mary's appointments with your teacher. Then ask your partner.

BOB'S APPOINTMENT:
1. Who is Bob's doctor? Dr. Lam.
2. When is Bob's next appointment?
3. What time is his next appointment?

MARY'S APPOINTMENT:
1. What time is Mary's appointment?
2. Who is her dentist?
3. What day is her appointment?

Measles

Mumps

Pair Practice: Ask and answer questions about Ahmad with your teacher and then with your partners. Ask your partners the same questions and write their answers on the chart. Use the example as a model.

EXAMPLE: A: Did Ahmad have the measles?   B: Yes.
          A: Did you have the measles?   B: Yes/No.

NAME	MEASLES	MUMPS	CHICKENPOX	SMALLPOX
Ahmad	yes	yes	no	yes
_____ (partner)				
_____ (partner)				

Pair Practice: Ask and answer questions about Ahmad with your teacher and then with your partners. Ask your partners the same questions and write their answers on the chart. Use the example as a model.

EXAMPLE: A: Did Ahmad have an immunization for DPT?   B: Yes.
          A: Did you have a vaccination for _____ ?   B: Yes/No.

IMMUNIZATIONS			VACCINATIONS	
Name	DPT	Polio	Smallpox	Measles
Ahmad	yes	no	yes	no
_____ (partner)				
_____ (partner)				

A NEW PATIENT

A: My name is Angela Ramirez.
   I have a 10:30 appointment.
B: You're a new patient, aren't you?
A: That's right.
B: Please take a seat and fill out this form.

PRACTICE

You're a new patient, aren't you?
He's/She's   isn't he/she?

Please fill out this form.
   in the health form.
complete the form.

Discuss the information on the following chart with your teacher and class.

HEALTH INFORMATION

Name __Wing   Barry__   Date __5-19-1990__
         Last   First

Address __1025   Logan Ave.__   Phone __660-7181__
         __Green River,   CA   92030__

         _____   (✓) M ☑ F ☐

ILLNESSES

Do you have problems with: (✓)

colds   ☑   heart   ☐
headaches   ☐   kidneys   ☐
stomachaches   ☐
                        Other _____

DISEASES

Did you have: (✓)

chickenpox   ☑   mumps   ☑
measles   ☐
                        Other _____

IMMUNIZATION/VACCINATION SHOTS

Were you vaccinated against: (✓)

TB   ☐   polio   ☑
smallpox   ☐
                        Other __tetanus__

YES/NO

Read each sentence. Circle yes or no after each sentence.

1. Barry has problems with headaches.   yes   no
2. He had the mumps.   yes   no
3. He had a smallpox vaccination.   yes   no

Use information about yourself to fill out the form.

HEALTH INFORMATION

Name _____   Date _____
      Last   First

Address _____   Phone _____

_____

_____   (✔) M ☐ F ☐

ILLNESSES

Do you have problems with: (✔)

colds ☐   heart ☐
headaches ☐   kidneys ☐
stomachaches ☐

Other _____

DISEASES

Did you have: (✔)

chickenpox ☐   mumps ☐
measles ☐

Other _____

IMMUNIZATION/VACCINATION SHOTS

Were you vaccinated against: (✔)

TB ☐   polio ☐
smallpox ☐

Other _____

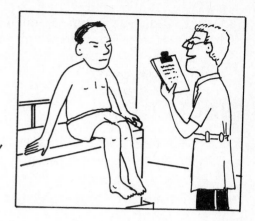

A: OK, Tony. Let's check you out. Open your mouth, and stick out your tongue. Say a-h-h-h.
B: A-h-h-h-h.
A: Inhale, exhale, inhale.
B: I'm sorry. I don't understand.
A: (demonstrates) Breathe in, breathe out, breathe in.
B: OK.

PRACTICE

Let's check you out.
    take a look.
      see.

Open your mouth.
Stick out your tongue.
Roll up your sleeve.
Take off your clothes.

I'm sorry, I don't understand.
Excuse me,
Repeat that, please.

Turn around.
Sit up.
Bend over.

Pair Practice: Follow the directions your teacher gives. Then give directions to your partner.

EXAMPLE: Inhale, exhale. (Partner demonstrates.)

Pair Practice: Ask and answer these questions with your teacher. Then ask your partner.

1. What can you say when you don't understand?
2. What do you usually do when you don't understand?

PRESCRIPTIONS

A: You need some medicine, Tony.
   Here's your prescription.
B: Thanks, Doctor. I'll take care of it
   right away.

PRACTICE

You need some medicine.
        a prescription.
        a shot
I'll take care of it right away.
    get it   now.
    fill it   tomorrow.

AT THE DRUGSTORE

A: Is my prescription ready?
B: Yes, here it is.
A: How many should I take?
B: One pill every four hours.
   It's on the label.
A: OK. One pill every four hours.
   I'll remember. Thanks a lot.

PRACTICE

How many should I take?
Take one pill every four hours.
      two capsules after meals.
      a tablet as needed.

How much should I take?
Take 1 teaspoon at bedtime.
          three times a day.
2 teaspoons before meals.
          after meals.

Pair Practice: Ask and answer these questions with your teacher. Then ask your partner.

1. Do you take prescription medicine?
2. Where do you fill the prescription?
3. What is the medicine for?
4. Where do people fill prescriptions in your country?

Pair Practice: Ask and answer the questions about each prescription with your teacher. Then ask your partner.

FED-MART PHARMACY

3249 Sports Arena Blvd.

No. 623,451   224-3683

Dr. Anderson

Than Nguyen   2/6/90

One tablet before meals.

QUESTIONS

1. Who wrote the prescription?
2. When should Than take a tablet?
3. What is the number of the prescription?
4. What is the name of the pharmacy?

DRUG MART

3056 Clairmont Drive

No. 536,120   276-2310

Dr. James Benson

Maria Garcia   6/2/90

Take two teaspoons every four hours
for cough.   Refill

QUESTIONS

1. Who is the prescription for?
2. How much medicine should she take?
3. Who is her doctor?
4. Can Maria get a refill?

NONPRESCRIPTION MEDICINE

A: My throat is very sore.
   Do you have a good cough medicine?
B: Yes, we do.
A: Great! Which one do you recommend?
B: I like No-Coff. I use it myself.
A: Sounds good. Where can I find it?
B: In section A on the top shelf.

PRACTICE

Which one do you recommend?
        suggest?
        like?
        use?

You can find it in section A.
        aisle 3.
        on the top shelf.

Pair Practice: Ask and answer these questions with your teacher. Then ask your partner.

1. Where can you buy nonprescription medicine?
2. Do you take nonprescription medicines?
    Which ones?
3. What do you take for a fever? a cold? a headache?

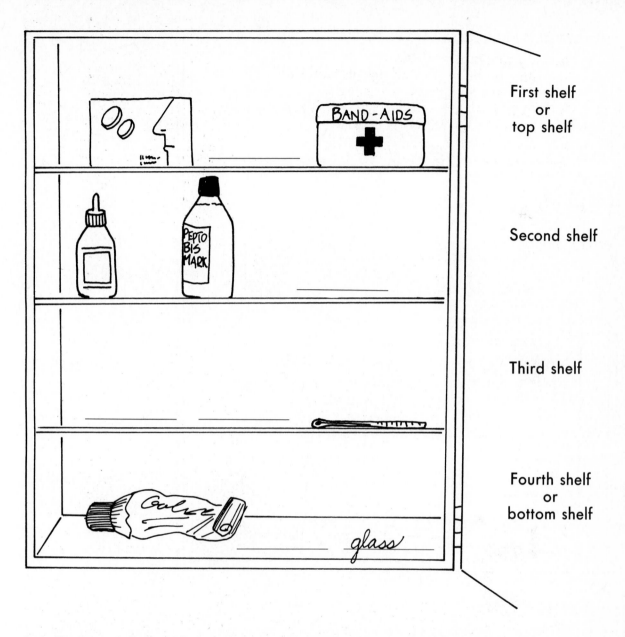

First shelf
or
top shelf

Second shelf

Third shelf

Fourth shelf
or
bottom shelf

Pair Practice: Ask and answer questions about items in the medicine cabinet with your teacher and then with your partner. Student A asks student B for information about items missing from Part A of the medicine cabinet and then writes in the word or draws a picture of the item in the correct space. Use the example as a model.

EXAMPLE: A: Where's the glass?
               B: It's on the bottom shelf on the right.
               A: Where are the eyedrops?

               B: They're on the _____ .

Ask B about: glass   cough syrup   aspirin   gauze   eyedrops   toothbrush

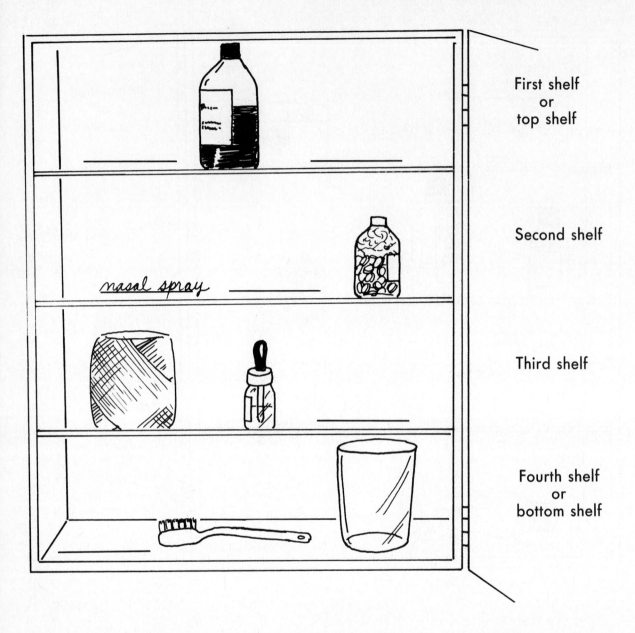

First shelf
or
top shelf

Second shelf

nasal spray _____

Third shelf

Fourth shelf
or
bottom shelf

Pair Practice: Ask and answer questions about items in the medicine cabinet with your teacher and then with your partner. Student B asks student A for information about items missing from Part B of the medicine cabinet and writes in the word or draws a picture of the item in the correct space. Use the example as a model.

EXAMPLE: B: Where's the nasal spray?
            A: It's on the second shelf on the left.
            B: Where are the cold tablets?

            A: They're on the _____ .

Ask A about: cold tablets   bandages   nasal spray   Pepto-Bismark
              thermometer   toothpaste

1. Where's the boy?
2. What's he doing?
3. Where's his mother?

1. What's he eating?
2. Should he eat it?
3. Why? Why not?

1. How does he feel?
2. How does she feel?
3. What can she do?

1. Where did she go?
2. Who did she talk to?
3. What did he say?

Pair Practice: Ask and answer these questions with your teacher. Then ask your partner.

1. Where do you keep your medicine?
2. If you have children, can they get to the medicine?

TAKE HIM TO EMERGENCY

A: Roberto! Vinh fell off his bike.
   I think he broke his arm.
B: Hurry! Take him to your doctor.
A: We don't have one.
B: Then take him to Emergency at the hospital.
   I'll go with you.
A: Thanks! Come on, Vinh, let's go!

PRACTICE

Take him to Emergency.
  her   Public Health.
          the hospital.
          clinic.
          doctor.

I'll go with you.
  dial 911.
  call the doctor.
        paramedics.

Pair Practice: Ask and answer questions with your teacher and then ask your classmates. Use the example as a model. Write the information in each box.

EXAMPLE: Did you go to Emergency? Yes, I did.
         Why?   I cut my foot.

Find Someone Who Went To . . .

EMERGENCY	PUBLIC HEALTH	CLINIC
Name _Jim_	Name _____	Name _____
Why? _He cut his foot_	Why? _____	Why? _____
HOSPITAL	DRUGSTORE	_____?_____
Name _____	Name _____	Name _____
Why? _____	Why? _____	Why? _____

A: (Dials 911 or operator) Help! My wife is unconscious!
B: What's your name?
A: Art Abebe.
B: What's your address?
A: 1415 Benton Way.
B: What's the nearest cross street?
A: Redding Avenue.
B: Stay on the line. Don't hang up.
A: OK.

PRACTICE

My father is choking.
My mother   bleeding.
The baby   drowning.

My neighbor's house is on fire.
My daughter drank poison.
           ate

Fill in the numbers for the area where you live.

EMERGENCY NUMBERS

EMERGENCY   _____

POLICE   _____

FIRE DEPARTMENT   _____

POISON CONTROL   _____

SHERIFF   _____

_____   _____

Pair Practice: Ask and answer questions with your teacher and then with your partner. Use the example as a model. Ask about Mrs. Luna, Jim, Lily, and your partner. Fill in the chart with the information about your partner.

EXAMPLE:
1. Who does Mrs. Luna call?   Poison Control.
2. What is the problem?   Her son ate rat poison.
3. What is her address?   223 Ash Street.
4. What is her cross street?   Third Avenue.

NAME	CALL	PROBLEM	ADDRESS	CROSS STREET
Mrs. Luna	Poison Control	Her son ate rat poison.	223 Ash Street	Third Avenue
Jim	911	His father is having a heart attack.	1122 Comet Way	Broadway
Lily	Police	Someone is in her house.	6 Rexford Drive	Magnolia
(your partner)	_____	_____	_____	_____

READING EXERCISE

Yesterday Mrs. Tam's daughter, Lila, was sick. Mrs. Tam took Lila's temperature. It was 102°. Mrs. Tam called the doctor. He told her to bring her daughter in. The doctor examined Lila. Then he wrote a prescription for her. Mrs. Tam went to the drugstore to get the medicine. The label stated, *Take one pill every four hours.* Lila feels fine now.

QUESTIONS

1. How was Lila yesterday?
2. Was Mrs. Tam sick, too?
3. What was Lila's temperature?
4. What did the doctor do?
5. Where did Mrs. Tam get the medicine?

YES/NO

Read each sentence. Circle yes or no after each sentence.

1. Mrs. Tam had a sore throat.	Yes	(No)
2. Her daughter's temperature was 102°.	Yes	No
3. Mrs. Tam called the pharmacist.	Yes	No
4. The label stated, *Take one pill every four hours.*	Yes	No
5. Lila feels fine now.	Yes	No

WRITE ABOUT YOURSELF

1. What do you do when you are sick? _____

_____

2. Do you stay at home? _____

_____

3. What medicine do you buy at the drugstore? _____

_____

chapter **4**

TRANSPORTATION

COMPETENCY OBJECTIVES

On completion of this chapter, the students will show orally, in writing, or through demonstration that they are able to use language needed in the following situations:

A. LOCAL TRANSPORTATION

- Use city buses to travel to and from school, shopping areas, jobs, and homes of friends.
- Call a taxi when needed.
- Walk safely in prescribed areas.
- Use self-service and full-service gas stations.

B. OUT-OF-TOWN TRANSPORTATION

- Buy a bus ticket to a designated city.
- Differentiate between one-way and round trip.
- Check and tag baggage.
- Inquire about lost luggage.

I WALK TO SCHOOL

A: How do you come to school?
B: I walk. I live around the corner.
A: Oh, I take the bus.
   I live a long way from here.

PRACTICE

I take the bus.
  ride my bicycle.
  drive my car.
I come by bus.
        car.
        bicycle.

I live a long way from here.
  far from here.
  around the corner.
  3 miles away.
  six blocks away.
  near here.
  near the park.

Pair Practice: Ask and answer these questions with your teacher. Then ask your partner.

1. Do you live near school?
2. How do you come to school?

CROSS AT THE CROSSWALK

A: Don't cross in the middle of the street.
B: Why not?
A: It's dangerous. Maybe you'll get a ticket.
   Cross at the crosswalk.
B: OK. Let's cross now. It says, WALK.

PRACTICE

Don't cross in the middle of the street.
         against the light.
         on a red light.
         when it says, DON'T WALK.

Cross at the crosswalk.
      at the corner.
      on the green light.
      in the pedestrian crossing.

Don't cross here.   Why not?   It's dangerous.
Don't smoke.   Why not?   It's not allowed.
Don't do that.   Why not?

Pair Practice: Ask and answer these questions with your teacher. Then ask your partner.

1. Where do you cross the street?
2. Do you follow traffic rules?
3. If you have children, do they know the rules?

Are they lost?
How do you know?
What does the police officer tell them?

What are they doing?
What will happen to them?

What is the police officer saying?
How do you think they feel?

Does the police officer give them a ticket?
Are they following the traffic rules?

Pair Practice: Ask and answer these questions with your teacher. Then ask your partner.

1. Do you ever ask for directions?
2. Can a police officer help you?

TAKING THE BUS

A: Watch your step.
B: Does this bus go downtown?
A: Yes, it does. Put your fare in the box.
B: How much is it?
A: Ninety-five cents. Exact change, please.

PRACTICE

Does this bus go downtown?
                 uptown?
                 to the train station?

How much is it?
What is the fare?

TRANSFER, PLEASE

A: How do I get to the West Side Shopping Center?
B: Take this bus downtown. Transfer to the number 34 bus.
A: Does it cost any more?
B: No, give this transfer to the other driver.
A: Thank you.

PRACTICE

How do I get to North Park?
               the East Side?
               the beach?
               City Adult School?

Tell me where to change buses.
                   catch the bus.
                   get on the bus.
                   get off the bus.

INTERVIEW

Do you ever ride the bus?
How much does it cost?
Do you change buses?
Did you ride the bus in your country?

CALLING A TAXI

A: ABC Cab.
B: Please send a cab to 4030 Felton Street.
A: What's the street?
B: Felton. F-E-L-T-O-N.
A: OK. We'll send one right away.

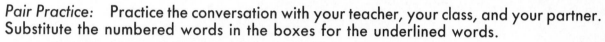

PRACTICE

Please send a cab.   We'll send one right away.
       driver.   now.
       taxi.   immediately.
                        at once.

Pair Practice: Practice the conversation with your teacher, your class, and your partner. Substitute the numbered words in the boxes for the underlined words.

A: Please send a cab to 2566 <u>Taylor</u> Street.
                        1

B: What's the street?
A: Taylor. <u>T-A-Y-L-O-R</u> .
             2

B: OK.

1. Monroe.	1. Thomas.	1. Leeds.	1. Valley.
2. M-O-N-R-O-E.	2. T-H-O-M-A-S.	2. L-E-E-D-S.	2. V-A-L-L-E-Y.

EXAMPLE: A: Please send a cab to 2566 <u>Monroe</u> Street.
          B: What's the street?
          A: Monroe. <u>M-O-N-R-O-E</u> .
          B: OK.

Pair Practice: Practice the conversation with your teacher, your class, and your partner. Substitute the numbers in the boxes for the underlined numbers.

A: Please send a cab to <u>3056</u> Pine Street.
                    1

B: <u>1356</u> Pine Street?
    2
A: No. <u>3056</u>.
      1

B: OK.

1. 1581	1. 4072	1. 8093	1. 6024
2. 5081	2. 1472	2. 1893	2. 1624

EXAMPLE: A: Please send a cab to 1581 Pine.
          B: <u>5081</u> Pine?
          A: No, <u>1581</u>.
          B: OK.

FILL IT UP!

A: Fill it up with unleaded, please.
B: OK. Should I check under the hood?
A: Please, and wash the windows, too.
B: Everything's fine.
   That'll be $14.50.
A: Here you are. Thank you.

PRACTICE

Should I check under the hood?
            the water and oil?
            the tires?
            the battery?

SELF-SERVICE

A: We need some gas.
B: Pull in here. I'll pump it.
A: Do we pay now or later?
B: Now. The sign says, *Pay cashier first.*

PRACTICE

We need some gas.   Pull in here.
         oil.   Go in
         water.   Turn in

Pair Practice: Ask and answer these questions with your teacher. Then ask your partner.

1. Do you go to self-service or full-service gas stations? Why?
2. Which is cheaper? Which is faster?

OUTSIDE the CAR

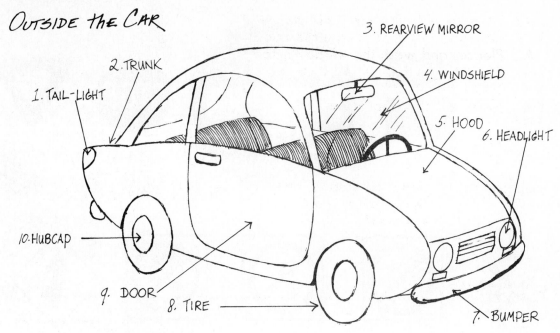

1. TAIL-LIGHT
2. TRUNK
3. REARVIEW MIRROR
4. WINDSHIELD
5. HOOD
6. HEADLIGHT
7. BUMPER
8. TIRE
9. DOOR
10. HUBCAP

INSIDE the CAR

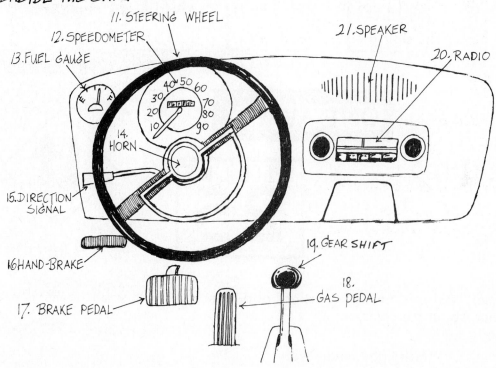

11. STEERING WHEEL
12. SPEEDOMETER
13. FUEL GAUGE
14. HORN
15. DIRECTION SIGNAL
16. HAND-BRAKE
17. BRAKE PEDAL
18. GAS PEDAL
19. GEAR SHIFT
20. RADIO
21. SPEAKER

Pair Practice: Talk about the parts of a car with your teacher and then with your partner. Which parts are inside the car? Which parts are outside the car? Do you know how to fix anything on a car?

Pair Practice: Ask and answer questions about the signs with your teacher. Then ask your partner about the signs.

EXAMPLE: 1. Which light means wait?
2. Can you walk now?
3. Can you go in here?

 _____

 _____

 _____

Write the letter of the correct meaning next to each sign.

A. Two lanes go into one lane (merge).

B. Railroad crossing

C. No U-turn

D. Pedestrians cross here (people walk across the street).

E. Don't go. Stop.

F. Let other cars go first (yield).

G. No left turn

 _____

 _____

I'D LIKE TWO TICKETS

A: May I help you?
B: Yes. How much is a ticket to Garden Center?
A: One-way or round-trip?
B: Round-trip.
A: It's $45 for round-trip.
B: OK. I'd like two tickets, please.

PRACTICE

How much is a ticket?
           one-way ticket?
           round-trip ticket?

Pair Practice: Student A asks student B for information missing from part A. Student B asks student A for information missing from part B. Practice with your teacher first. Then practice with your partner.

PART A			PART B		
Town	One-way	Round-trip	Town	One-way	Round-trip
Greenfield	$25.00	?	Greenfield	?	$45.00
Garden Center	?	$66.00	Garden Center	$36.00	?
Hillside	?	$250.00	Hillside	$138.00	?
Pine Grove	$55.00	?	Pine Grove	?	$100.00

EXAMPLE:

STUDENT A

1. How much is a round-trip ticket to Greenfield?

STUDENT B

1. $45.00

LOST LUGGAGE

A: Excuse me. I just arrived from Garden Center,
   and my luggage isn't here.
B: Did you check the baggage claim office?
A: Yes, I did. It's not there.
B: Give me your name and a local phone number.
   We'll call you when it gets in.
A: I hope it's soon.

PRACTICE

Did you check the baggage claim office?
                lost and found?
                customer service office?

Pair Practice: Ask and answer these questions with your teacher. Then ask your partner.

1. Did your luggage ever get lost?
2. Did you find it?
3. Was everything there?

READING EXERCISE

Ann comes to school by bus. She lives a long way from school. She waits for the bus at the bus stop near her house. When she gets on the bus, she puts her fare in the box. The fare is 95¢. She has the exact change. Sometimes she goes downtown. Then she needs a transfer to change buses.

QUESTIONS

1. How does Ann come to school?
2. Where does she wait for the bus?
3. Where does she put the fare?
4. Why does she need a transfer?

YES/NO

Read each sentence. Circle yes or no after each sentence.

1. Ann walks to school.   Yes   (No)
2. She lives a long way from school.   Yes   No
3. The fare is $1.05.   Yes   No
4. Sometimes Ann goes downtown.   Yes   No

WRITE ABOUT YOURSELF

1. How do you come to school? _____

_____

2. Do you live far from school? _____

_____

3. Do you ride a bicycle? _____

_____

4. Do you drive a car? _____

_____

HOUSING

COMPETENCY OBJECTIVES

On completion of this chapter, the students will show orally, in writing, or through demonstration that they are able to use language needed in the following situations:

A. LOCATE HOUSING

- Identify types of housing.
- Read housing ads.
- Express housing needs.
- Explain deposit requirements.

B. IDENTIFY ROOMS AND ITEMS IN A HOUSE

- Identify and name the rooms in a house.
- Identify and name common items in a house.
- Identify sources for used and less expensive items.

C. HOUSING REGULATIONS

- State basic tenant and landlord rules and responsibilities.
- Identify sources for assistance in problem solving.

D. MAINTENANCE AND REPAIR

- Identify, describe, and report basic household problems.
- Describe household problems and request repairs.
- Identify and name common tools.
- Identify and name basic household cleaning equipment.

READING THE ADS

A: Did you see this ad for a studio?
B: Yes, I did. But I don't understand *utils pd.*
A: It means you don't pay for the gas and lights.
B: Oh, that's good! Let's go look at it.

PRACTICE

Did you see this ad?
     read
     find

Yes, I did.
No, he/she didn't.

I don't understand *utils pd.*
     w/w cpts.
     lndry rm.

Housing Abbreviations

Pair Practice: Ask and answer questions about each abbreviation with your teacher and then with your partner. Draw a line from each abbreviation to the correct meaning.

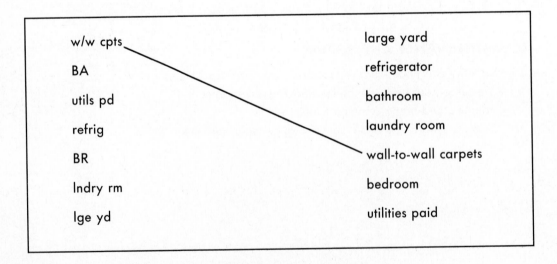

EXAMPLE: A: What does *w/w cpts* mean?
             B: It means *wall-to-wall carpets.*

1

```
          Apartment for Rent
$625                              2BR
Utils pd, refrig, stove
lndry rm   No pets
Call 9–6 pm              230-2969
```

Apartment

2

```
$850                       3 BR house
1½ BA        lge yard
w/w cpts     New paint
After 5:30 pm            617-9342
```

House

3

```
Studio        $325
1 quiet adult     utils pd
Available 11/1      Call 224-5763
```

Studio

Pair Practice: Ask and answer questions about each ad with your teacher. Then ask your partner.

EXAMPLE: **1.**   How much is the rent for the apartment? $625.
　　　　　　2.   How many bedrooms does it have?
　　　　　　3.   Are the utilities paid?
　　　　　　4.   What number do you call?

LOOKING AT THE CLASSIFIEDS

A: What are you looking at?
B: The classifieds. I have to move.
A: Are you looking for a house or an apartment?
B: I need a house or a two-bedroom apartment.

PRACTICE

I have to move.
           leave.
           go.

What are you looking at?   The classifieds.
                                   The want ads.
                                   A bulletin board.

I need a house.
          three bedrooms.
          an apartment.

Are you looking for a house or an apartment?
                       studio or a duplex?

Pair Practice: Ask and answer these questions with your teacher. Then ask your partner.

1. Do you live in a house or an apartment?
2. How did you find it?
3. Do you like where you live?
4. Why? Why not?

RENTING AN APARTMENT

A: How much is the rent?
B: It's $575. You pay the first and last month's rent and a $75.00 cleaning deposit.
A: A cleaning deposit? What's that?
B: Money you get back if the apartment is clean when you move out.
A: OK. We'll think about it.

PRACTICE

You pay the cleaning deposit.
    water.
    gas and lights.
    utilities.
    first and last month's rent.
It's money you get back.
    returned.
    refunded.

Apartment or House?

Pair Practice: Ask and answer questions about Maria with your teacher and then with your partners. Use the example as a model.

EXAMPLE: Does Maria live in an apartment? Yes.
      Does Maria live in a house?   No.

Ask your partners the same questions. Fill in the chart with the information about your partners.

1. Do you live in an apartment or a house?
2. Is it close to school?
3. How many bedrooms does it have?
4. Did you pay a cleaning deposit?
5. Did you pay the first and last month's rent when you moved in?

NAME	APARTMENT?	HOUSE?	CLOSE TO SCHOOL?	HOW MANY BEDROOMS?	CLEANING DEPOSIT?	FIRST AND LAST MONTH'S RENT?
Maria	yes	no	no	2	yes	yes
_____ (partner)						
_____ (partner)						

Mr. and Mrs. Adani looked for a one-bedroom apartment. They didn't find one, but they did find a studio apartment. It has one large room with a kitchen/dining room area. It has a couch that opens to make a bed. The rent is $350 a month including utilities. The landlord wants a $75 cleaning deposit. The Adanis will get the deposit back if the apartment is clean when they move out.

QUESTIONS

1. What kind of apartment did Mr. and Mrs. Adani look for?
2. What did they find?
3. What is a studio apartment?

YES/NO

Read each sentence. Circle yes or no after each sentence.

1. Mr. and Mrs. Adani needed a one-bedroom apartment.	(Yes)	No
2. They rented a studio apartment.	Yes	No
3. The rent is $450 a month.	Yes	No
4. The cleaning deposit is $75.	Yes	No
5. The Adanis will get the deposit back if the apartment is clean when they move out.	Yes	No

WRITE ABOUT YOURSELF

1. Do you live in an apartment or a house? _____

_____

2. Do you rent the apartment (house)? _____

_____

3. List the rooms in your apartment (house). _____

_____

1.

2.

3.

4.

5.

6.

7.

8.

9.

10.

11.

12.

Pair Practice: Ask and answer questions about each picture with your teacher and then with your partner.

EXAMPLE: A: Do you have a chair in your house?   B: Yes, I do.
                    A: Which room is it in?   B: It's in the living
                                                                                             room.

| chair | table | couch | bed | chest of drawers | refrigerator |
| lamp | toilet | bathtub | rug | TV | stove |

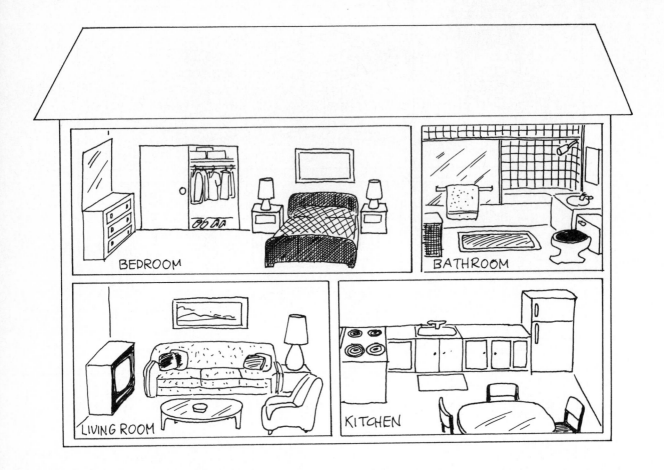

Pair Practice: Ask and answer these questions with your teacher. Then ask your partner.

EXAMPLE:
1. What rooms are in the house?
2. What do you do in each room?
3. What is in each room?
4. What do you have in your house?
5. What do you need to buy for your house?

GARAGE SALE

A: Hey, the neighbors are having a garage sale.
B: Did you see a chair there?
A: Yes, and it's better than the one at the swap meet.
B: Great! I hope it's cheaper, too!

Pair Practice: Practice the following conversations with your teacher and then with your partner. Substitute the numbered words in the boxes for the underlined words in the conversation.

EXAMPLE: A: Did you see a <u>sofa</u> there?
                                          1
            B: Yes, and it's <u>cheaper than</u> the one at the <u>furniture store</u>.
                                          2   3

1. sofa	1. jacket	1. baby bed
2. cheaper than	2. nicer than	2. smaller than
3. furniture store	3. Bargain Town	3. flea market

Pair Practice: Ask your partner these questions.

1. Do you ever go to flea markets?
2. What can you buy there?
3. Did you have swap meets in your country?

1.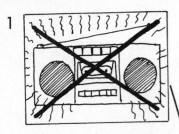

PUT OUT TRASH BY 7 A.M.

2.

NO CARS ON GRASS

3.

NO NOISE AFTER 10 P.M.

4.

NO BARBECUE INSIDE

5.

NO PETS

Pair Practice: Ask and answer questions about each picture with your teacher and then with your partner. Then draw a line from each picture to the correct rule.

EXAMPLE: A: Tell me about picture 1. What does it mean?
B: No noise after 10 P.M.

INTERVIEW

Do you have tenant rules where you live?
What kind?

NO PETS

A: If that dog is yours, I can't rent to you.
B: Why not?
A: We don't allow pets here.
   I'm sorry.
B: I'm sorry, too.

PRACTICE

We don't allow pets here.
              dogs

That dog is yours.
              mine.

No pets allowed.
   cats
   dogs

QUIET!

A: Hey! Turn down that music.
   I'm trying to sleep.
B: What time is it?
A: It's 11:30. No loud noise after 10:00 P.M.
B: All right! All right!

PRACTICE

Turn down the music.
   up   TV.
   off   radio.
   on   VCR.

I'm trying to sleep.
           relax.
           rest.
           read.

1

GIVE 30-DAY NOTICE OF RULE CHANGES

2

GIVE WRITTEN RECEIPTS FOR RENT PAYMENT

3

KEEP BUILDING AND GROUNDS CLEAN

Pair Practice: Ask and answer questions about each picture with your teacher and then with your partner. Then draw a line from each picture to the correct rule.

EXAMPLE:
1. Which picture shows the rent receipt?
   How much is the rent?
2. What is the landlord doing in picture 2?
3. What does the notice say in picture 3?
   How long can visitors stay?

INTERVIEW

Do you have landlord rules where you live? What kind?

INFORMATION HOT LINE

A: Hello, Information Hot Line. Can I help you?
B: I hope so. I moved, and the landlord won't return my deposit. What should I do?
A: Call Legal Aid, 546-7080.
   They can help you.
B: Thank you very much!

PRACTICE

What should I do?
            say?
            write
Who   call?
            talk to?

Call Legal Aid.
Talk to your friend.
            Information Hot Line.
            the Housing Bureau.
            a lawyer.

Who Should I Call?

Pair Practice: Ask and answer questions with your teacher and then with your partner. Use the example as a model. Ask about Tom, Sen, Bert and your partner. Fill in the chart with information about your partner.

NAME	PROBLEM WITH	PROBLEM	CALL
Tom	landlord	didn't return deposit	Information Hot Line
Sen	manager	doesn't give rent receipts	Housing Bureau
Bert	neighbor	hit my car	Legal Aid
Partner	?	?	?

EXAMPLE: A: Who has a problem?   B: Tom.
A: Who does he have a problem with?   B: His landlord.
           B: The landlord didn't return his deposit.
A: What's the problem?
A: Who should he call?   B: Information Hot Line.

IMPORTANT TELEPHONE NUMBERS

Fill in the numbers for the area where you live.

Information Hot Line _____   Legal Aid _____

Housing Bureau _____   (Other) _____

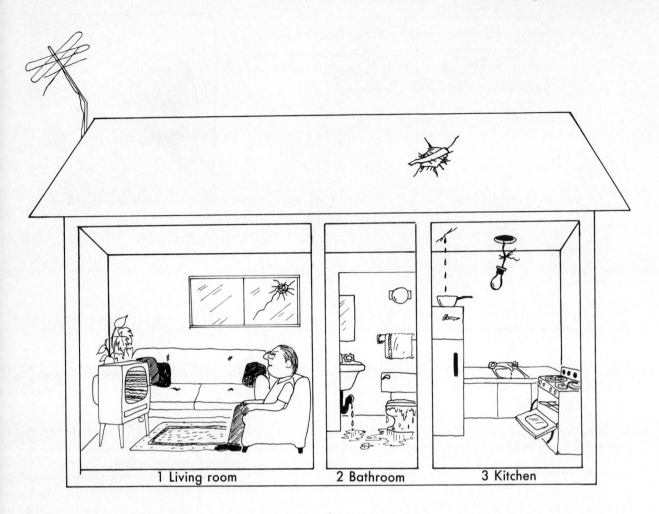

1 Living room   2 Bathroom   3 Kitchen

Pair Practice: Ask and answer questions about the problems in each room in the house with your teacher and then with your partner. Use the example as a model.

EXAMPLE: **1.**   What is wrong in the living room? The window is broken.
           2.   Who can fix it?

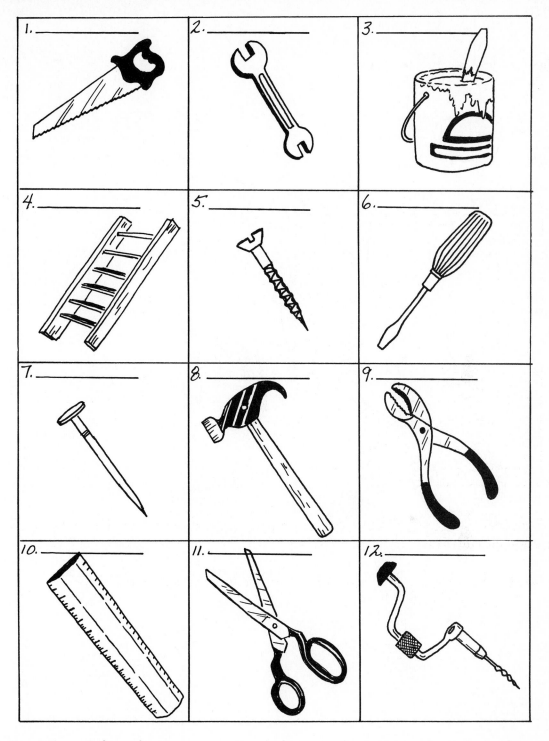

1. _____
2. _____
3. _____
4. _____
5. _____
6. _____
7. _____
8. _____
9. _____
10. _____
11. _____
12. _____

Pair Practice: Ask and answer questions about each picture with your teacher. Then ask your partner.

EXAMPLE: **1.** Do you have a saw?

          2. What can you use it for?

| saw | wrench | paintbrush | ladder | screw | screwdriver |
| hammer | pliers | ruler | scissors | drill | nail |

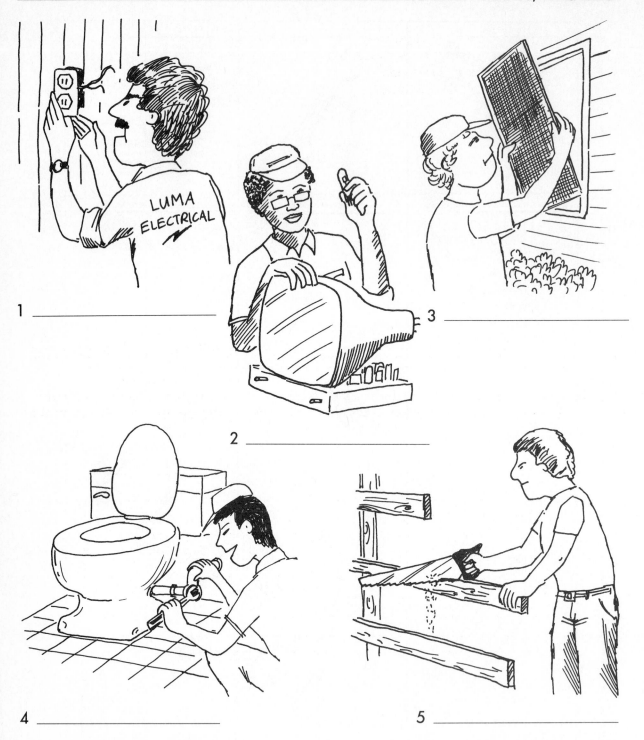

1 _____

2 _____

3 _____

4 _____

5 _____

Pair Practice: Ask and answer questions about each picture with your teacher. Then ask your partner.

EXAMPLE: 1. What can the electrician do? He can fix your lights.
          2. What else can he do?

electrician   TV repairperson   handyman   plumber   carpenter

96

CALL THE PLUMBER

A: My sink is still stopped up.
B: Did you try drain cleaner?
A: Yes, I tried it last week.
B: OK. I'll call the plumber.

PRACTICE

My sink is still stopped up.
            overflowing.
            broken.
Did you try drain cleaner?
       use

I told you last week.
He/She called him/her yesterday.
We asked them this morning.
I'll tell.
He'll/She'll call.
We'll ask.

Problems in the House

Pair Practice: Practice the following conversations with your teacher and then with your partner. Substitute the numbered words in the boxes for the underlined words in the conversation.

1. toilet overflowing	1. window broken	1. TV sparking
2. plunger	2. putty	2. the cable box
3. yesterday	3. last month	3. this morning
4. plumber	4. handyman	4. TV repairperson

EXAMPLE: A: My <u>toilet is still overflowing</u>.
                                1
             B: Did you try <u>a plunger</u>?
                             2

A: Yes, I tried it <u>yesterday</u>.
                      3
B: OK. I'll call <u>a plumber</u>.
                     4

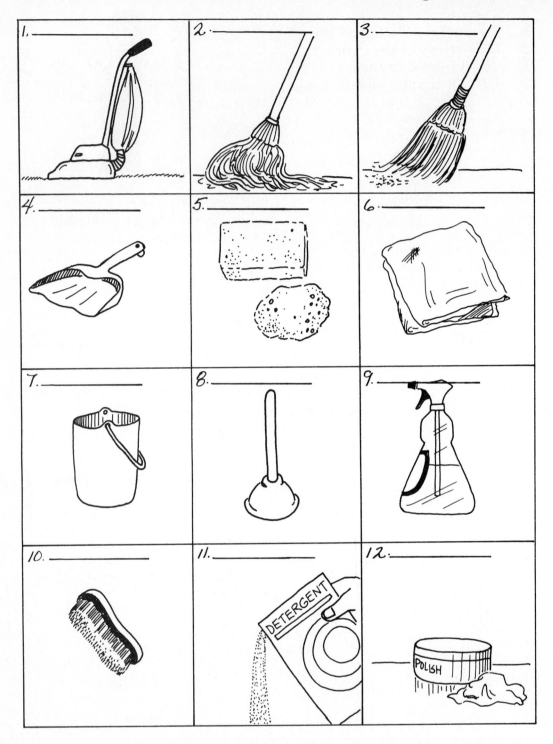

1. _____
2. _____
3. _____
4. _____
5. _____
6. _____
7. _____
8. _____
9. _____
10. _____
11. _____
12. _____

Pair Practice: Ask and answer questions about each picture with your teacher. Then ask your partner.

EXAMPLE: A: What do you clean with a vacuum?   B: My living room rug.
A: How do you use a vacuum cleaner?

vacuum	mop	dustpan	sponge	dustcloth	bucket
window cleaner	broom	brush	detergent/soap	polish/wax	plunger

I JUST MOPPED THE FLOOR

A: Be careful. Don't slip.
   I just mopped the floor.
B: Oh! It really shines.
   What did you use to clean it?
A: I used Super Floor Cleaner.
   Then I waxed it with Shine Bright.
B: I'm going to use them on
   my floor, too!

PRACTICE

I just mopped.
    waxed
    polished.
    washed.
    vacuumed.
    dusted.
    swept.

I used a mop.
    cloth.
    sponge.
    vacuum.
    rag.
    window cleaner.
    polish.
    wax.

I'm going to use it.
    them.
He's/She's going to try it.
    buy

Cleaning The House

Pair Practice: Ask and answer these questions with your teacher. Then ask your partner. Share your answers with the rest of the class.

EXAMPLE:
1. Who does the cleaning at your house?
2. Do you like to clean house? Why? Why not?
3. Do you think men should (should not) clean house?
4. Do you think children should clean house?
5. Who cleaned the house in your country?

1. Where is the little girl?
2. What is she doing?
3. Where is her mother?

1. What happened?
2. Is the little girl happy?
3. Is her mother happy?

1. What is the mother doing?
2. Who did she call?
3. What is he saying?

1. Who is the man?
2. What did he do?
3. What did the mother do?

Pair Practice: Ask and answer these questions with your teacher. Then ask your partner.

EXAMPLE: 1.   Did your toilet ever overflow?
2. What did you do?
3. Do you call a plumber sometimes? What for?

Lisa, age five, lives in an apartment with her mother. One morning, Lisa played in the toilet with her toy duck. The toilet stopped up, and the water overflowed. Lisa's mother called the building manager. The manager couldn't fix it. He called the plumber. Lisa's mother paid the plumber $50. Lisa doesn't play in the toilet any more.

QUESTIONS

1. Where does Lisa live?
2. Did Lisa play in the bedroom?
3. What stopped up and overflowed?
4. Who fixed the toilet?
5. How much did Lisa's mother pay?

YES/NO

Read each sentence. Circle yes or no after each sentence.

1. Lisa's mother played in the toilet.   Yes   (No)
2. The toilet stopped up.   Yes   No
3. Lisa's mother was happy.   Yes   No
4. The manager paid the plumber.   Yes   No
5. Lisa's mother paid $50.   Yes   No

WRITE ABOUT YOURSELF

1. Did you ever have anything fixed in your house? _____

   _____

2. What was it? _____

3. Who fixed it? _____

chapter 6

CLOTHING

COMPETENCY OBJECTIVES

On completion of this chapter, the students will show orally, in writing, or through demonstration that they are able to use language needed in the following situations:

A. CLOTHING

- Identify common articles of clothing.
- Express clothing shopping needs.
- Describe locations of clothing departments in a store.
- Describe clothing in terms of size, color, and price.
- Make and receive compliments about clothing.
- Interpret information on clothing labels.
- Interpret clothing care instructions.

B. PURCHASING PROCEDURES

- Use cash, a charge card, or a check to purchase clothing items.
- Exchange or return an item of clothing.

NEW CLOTHES

A: I need some new clothes.
   My children need new clothes, too.
B: What do you need?
A: I need a skirt. Tommy needs shoes,
   and Helen needs a dress.
B: Let's go shopping on Sunday.
   My kids need some new clothes, too.

PRACTICE

Tommy needs shoes
He   pants.
She   jeans.
            socks.

I need shoes.
We   pants
They jeans.
      socks.

Tommy needs a pair of shoes.
He   pants.
She   jeans.
                socks.

Pair Practice: Ask and answer these questions with your teacher. Then ask your partner.

1. What new clothes do you need?
2. If you have children, what new clothes do they need?
3. Where do you buy your clothes?
4. Do you make some of your clothes?

Pair Practice: Ask and answer questions about the clothing in each picture with your teacher. Then ask your partner.

EXAMPLE: **1.** Do you have a jacket?
              2. Do you need boots?

jacket	coat	boots	raincoat	sweater	hat	glasses	vest
pants	blouse	skirt	shorts	belt	tie	shoes	socks

1. _____
2. _____
3. _____
4. _____
5. _____
6. _____
7. _____
8. _____
9. _____
10. _____
11. _____
12. _____
13. _____
14. _____
15. _____
16. _____

Pair Practice: Ask and answer questions about the clothing in each picture with your teacher. Then ask your partner.

EXAMPLE: 1. Do you need to buy a shirt?
              2. Do you have slippers?

shirt	T-shirt	undershorts	pajamas	panties	bra
slip	bathrobe	necklace/earrings	purse	wallet	slippers
suit	watch	dress	umbrella		

A: You look very nice today.
Is that a new dress?
B: Yes, it is.
Do you like it?
A: It's beautiful.
B: Thanks.
A: You look very nice today.
Are those new pants?
B: Yes, they are.
Do you like them?
A: They're really nice.
B: Thank you. I think so,
too.

PRACTICE

Is that a new dress?
shirt?
sweater?
Are those new pants?
shoes?
glasses?

1. nice

2. really nice

3. beautiful

4. pretty

5. terrific

6. gorgeous

7. very handsome

Pair Practice: Ask and answer questions about the clothing in each picture with your teacher and then with your partner. Use the words in the right-hand column to describe each item.

EXAMPLE:
A: Is that a new *dress*?
B: Yes, it is.
A: It's *nice*.
B: Thank you.

A: Are those new *pants*?
B: Yes, they are.
A: They're *really nice*.
B: Thanks; I think so, too.

dress   pants   earrings   sweater   suit   skirt   boots

WHERE'S THE SHOE DEPARTMENT

A: Where's the shoe department?
B: It's on the second floor,
   in the middle on your left.

PRACTICE

Where's the shoe department?   It's on the first floor.
    women's   second
    men's   third
    children's   fourth
It's in the front.   your left.
    middle.   right.
    back.

The Department Store

Pair Practice: Practice the following conversations with your teacher and then with your partner. Substitute the numbered words in the boxes for the underlined words in the conversation.

1. men's	1. furniture	1. children's	1. toy	1. coffee shop
2. middle	2. front	2. back	2. middle	2. middle
3. left	3. right	3. right	3. back	3. front

EXAMPLE: A: Where's the <u>men's department</u>?
                   1
          B: It's in the <u>middle</u> on your <u>left</u>.
                     2   3

IN THE DEPARTMENT STORE

A: May I help you?
B: Yes. I'm looking for a blouse.
A: What size do you need?
B: Medium.
A: What color do you want?
B: Green.

PRACTICE

What size do you wear?
     want?
     need?

Size extra-small
  small
  medium
  large
  extra-large

What color do you like?
     want?
     need?

What are you looking for?
I'm looking for a blouse.
    skirt.
    sweater.
    dress.

I'm looking for pants.
    shoes.
    pajamas.
    shorts.

ITEM	SIZE	COLOR
	$10\frac{1}{2}$	bROWN

Pair Practice: Ask and answer questions about the clothing in each picture with your teacher. Then ask your partner. Write the answers on the chart.

EXAMPLE: 1. What are you looking for? Shoes.
            2. What size do you need? $10\frac{1}{2}$.
            3. What color do you want? Brown.

IT'S TOO TIGHT

A: How does that fit?
B: I like the color, but it's too tight.
A: That was a size 8. Why don't you try on a size 10?
B: This is perfect.

PRACTICE

It's too tight.
     loose.
     large.

This is perfect.
     terrific.
     fine.
     great.
     just right.

The color is too dark.
              light.

AN EXCHANGE

A: I bought this shirt for my father, but it's too small.
B: Do you have the receipt?
A: Yes, here it is.
B: Do you want to exchange it, or do you want a refund?
A: I'd like to exchange it for a bigger size.

PRACTICE

It's too small.
     big.
     long.
     short.

I'd like a bigger size.
     smaller
     shorter one.
     longer

Pair Practice: Look at the shirts. Ask your partner these questions.

EXAMPLE: A: What size is shirt 3?
                 B: Large.

1 small   2 medium   3 large   4 extra large

1. What size is shirt 3?
2. What size is shirt 4?
3. What size is shirt 1?
4. What size is shirt 2?
5. What size is your shirt?

1

2

Both partners look at picture 1. Student A asks student B these questions.
EXAMPLE: A: How does the shirt fit?
                 B: It's too small.
1. How does the shirt fit?
2. How does the hat fit?
3. How do the pants fit?
4. How do your clothes fit?

Both partners look at picture 2. Student B asks student A these questions.
EXAMPLE: B: How do the pants fit?
                 A: They're too big.
1. How does the hat fit?
2. How does the shirt fit?
3. How do the pants fit?
4. How does your shirt fit?

TWO IDs, PLEASE

A: That'll be $19.02.
B: I'm going to write a check.
A: I'll need to see two IDs.
B: I have my driver's license and a credit card.
A: That's fine. Here's your receipt.

PRACTICE

I'm going to write a check.
             pay by check.
I'll write a check.
   pay by check.
I have my driver's license and a credit card.
       student ID   state ID card.
       charge card
       visa

Pair Practice: Ask and answer these questions with your teacher. Then ask your partner.

1. Do you have ID?
2. How many IDs do you have?
3. What kind of ID do you have?
4. Do you have a credit card?
5. What credit card do you have?
6. Do you write checks?

HOW MUCH IS THIS SWEATER?

A: How much is this sweater?
B: It's $17.99 plus tax.
A: Fine. I'll take it.
B: Cash or charge?
A: Cash. I don't have a charge account here.
B: OK. Here's your receipt.

PRACTICE

How much is this sweater?
            skirt?
            blouse?

It's $17.99.

How much are these shoes?
             pants?
             jackets?

They're $21.99.

Cash or charge?

Cash.
I'll pay cash.
      charge it.
      write a check.
      use my credit card.

Pair Practice: Ask and answer these questions with your teacher. Then ask your partner.

1. Do you pay with cash?
2. Do you have a charge card or credit card?
3. How often do you use your credit card?
4. Where do you buy your clothes?

A.

1. _$12.99_   cash

2. _____ charge

3. _____ cash

4. _____ cash

5. _____ charge

6. _____ cash

7. _____ charge

8. _____ charge

9. _____ cash

10. _____ cash

B.

1. $12.99   cash or charge

2. $12.50   cash or charge

3. $25.00   cash or charge

4. $17.50   cash or charge

5. $7.95   cash or charge

6. $47.75   cash or charge

7. $78.60   cash or charge

8. $21.37   cash or charge

9. $6.95   cash or charge

10. $3.17   cash or charge

Pair Practice: Student A asks student B for information about each item in Part A and writes the correct price next to each item in Part A. Student B asks student A for information about Part B and circles *cash* or *charge* for each item in Part B. Use the example as a model.

EXAMPLE: A: How much is this sweater?
                 B: $12.99.
                 B: Cash or charge?
                 A: Cash.

A: Look! J-Mart is having a sale.
B: Those pants were $25 last week. Is there a sale today?
A: Yes. They're $15.95 now. That's a great buy!

PRACTICE

Those pants were $25 last week.
    dresses
    shoes
    shirts

They're $15.95 now.

That skirt was $19 last week.
    sweater
    jacket

It's $12.99 now.

That's a great buy.
    good
    good deal.
    bargain.

That's a good buy.
    better buy.
    the best buy.

Pair Practice: Ask and answer these questions with your teacher. Then ask your partner.

1. What are some local stores that have good sales on clothes?
2. Do you buy clothes when they are on sale?

_____ SHOPPING FOR CLOTHES

Mrs. Park takes the children shopping before school starts. Tommy needs shoes and pants. Helen needs a dress. The children try on their clothes in the store. They want their clothes to fit. Sometimes, when clothes don't fit, they have to return them. They get a refund, or they exchange them. Mrs. Park likes to buy clothes on sale to save money.

QUESTIONS

1. When does Mrs. Park take the children shopping?
2. What does Tommy need?
3. What does Helen need?
4. How do they know the clothes will fit?
5. Why does Mrs. Park like to buy clothes on sale?

YES/NO

Read each sentence. Circle yes or no after each sentence.

1. Mrs. Park goes shopping before school starts.   Yes   No
2. The children try on their clothes in the store.   Yes   No
3. They want their clothes to fit.   Yes   No
4. The children give away new clothes that don't fit.   Yes   No
5. Mrs. Park likes to buy clothes on sale.   Yes   No

WRITE ABOUT YOURSELF

1. Do you like to go shopping for clothes? _____

_____

2. What do you like to buy? _____

_____

3. Do you try on the clothes in the store? _____

_____

4. When do you exchange clothes? _____

_____

5. Why do you buy clothes on sale? _____

_____

1. Machine Wash
2. _____
3. _____
4. _____
5. _____
6. _____
7. _____
8. _____

Pair Practice: Ask and answer questions about each picture with your teacher and then with your partner. Use the example as a model. Then write the words in the correct box.

EXAMPLE: 1. Which picture shows Machine wash?

machine wash	hand wash	dry clean	cool iron
tumble dry	dry flat	line dry	cool water

READING LABELS

A: This sweater is too small now.
B: Did you wash it?
A: Yes, I did. Why?
B: Look at the label. It says, *dry clean only.*

PRACTICE

Look at the label.
    tag.
    instructions.

Read the label.
    tag.
    instructions.

It says, *dry clean only.*
    hand wash.
    cool water.
    cool iron.
    machine wash.
    tumble dry.
    line dry.
    dry flat.

Pair Practice: Ask and answer these questions with your teacher. Then ask your partner.

1. Do you wash sweaters at home?
2. Do you go to the dry cleaners?
3. Do you think dry cleaning is expensive? Why?
4. What clothes do you hand wash?
5. What clothes do you line dry?
6. What clothes do you tumble dry?

Pair Practice: Look at the three pictures. Ask and answer the questions with your teacher. Then ask your partner.

1. What time is it?
2. Where is the boy?
3. What is he doing?
4. How does he feel?

1. What time is it?
2. Who is the woman?
3. What is she doing?
4. What happened?

1. What time is it?
2. What is the woman saying?
3. How does she feel?
4. How does the boy feel?
5. What can the boy do?

_____ CLOTHING

On Saturday morning, Mrs. Benson washed clothes. Tommy put his mother's favorite sweater in the washing machine. When the wash finished, Mrs. Benson opened the washing machine to take out the clothes. Her sweater was too small. Mrs. Benson was very angry with Tommy. She told him to read labels carefully before putting clothes in the washing machine.

QUESTIONS

1. What did Mrs. Benson do on Saturday morning?
2. What did Tommy put in the washing machine?
3. Was the sweater too small or too large?
4. Who was angry with Tommy?
5. What does Tommy need to read?

YES/NO

Read each sentence. Circle yes or no after each sentence.

1. Mrs. Benson did the wash on Monday morning.   Yes   (No)
2. Tommy put socks in the washing machine.   Yes   No
3. The sweater was too small.   Yes   No
4. Mrs. Benson was very happy.   Yes   No
5. Tommy needs to read labels carefully.   Yes   No

WRITE ABOUT YOURSELF

1. Do you wash clothes in a washing machine or by hand? _____

   _____

2. Do you wash your clothes at home, or do you go to a laundromat?

   _____

3. Do you have to dry clean or hand wash some of your clothes? _____

   _____

4. Where do you take your clothes to be dry cleaned? _____

   _____

chapter 7

LOOKING FOR AND KEEPING A JOB

COMPETENCY OBJECTIVES

On completion of this chapter, the students will show orally, in writing, or through demonstration that they are able to use language needed in the following situations:

A. LOOKING FOR A JOB

- Interpret want ads relating to employment.
- Interpret want ad abbreviations.
- Ask about training at a skills center.
- Telephone to set up an employment interview.

B. INTERVIEWING FOR A JOB

- Ask questions concerning duties, hours, salary, and fringe benefits.
- Make follow-up call.

C. GETTING AND KEEPING A JOB

- Explain payroll deductions.
- Participate in a job performance review.

D. FILLING OUT A JOB APPLICATION

- Interpret a job application.
- Complete a job application.

THE WANT ADS

A: I'm looking for a job.
B: What kind of work are you looking for?
A: In my country, I was a mechanic.
   I want to do the same thing here.
B: Why don't you look in the newspaper?

PRACTICE

What kind of work are you looking for?
        job
        tools

I was a mechanic.
He/She waiter.
      fisherman.
      cook.

Why don't you look in the newspaper?
        ask your friends?
        go to the employment office?
        check the bulletin board?
Were you a secretary?
        student?
        nurse?

Pair Practice: Practice the following conversations with your teacher and then with your partner. Substitute the numbered words in the boxes for the underlined words in the conversations.

A: I'm looking for a job.
B: What kind?
A: In my country, I was a <u>mechanic</u>.
                         1
B: Why don't you <u>look in the newspaper</u>?
                         2

| 1. fisherman | 1. teacher | 1. secretary |
| 2. ask your friends | 2. go to the personnel office | 2. go to the employment office |

| 1. cashier | 1. cook | 1. gardener |
| 2. look in the want ads | 2. look for *Help Wanted* signs | 2. check the bulletin board |

EXAMPLE: A: I'm looking for a job.
           B: What kind of job are you looking for?
           A: In my country, I was a <u>fisherman</u>.
                                1
           B: Why don't you <u>ask your friends</u>?
                          2

INTERVIEW

What was your job in your country?
How did you get it?
Do you want to do that in the United States?

1 police officer
2 firefighter
3 fisherman
4 mail carrier
5 doctor nurse
6 homemaker

Pair Practice: Ask and answer questions about these occupations with your teacher and your class. Then ask your partner.

EXAMPLE: 1. What does a police officer do?
2. Do you want to be a police officer? Why? Why not?

police officer
firefighter

fisherman
mail carrier

doctor/nurse
homemaker

Pair Practice: Ask and answer questions about these occupations with your teacher and your class. Then ask your partner.

EXAMPLE: **1.**   What does a secretary do?
          2.   Do you want to be a secretary? Why? Why not?

secretary   seamstress/tailor   welder
cook/chef   mechanic   dentist

ABBREVIATIONS

1. wpm   a. required
2. sal   b. words per minute
3. exp   c. salary
4. req   d. benefits
5. bnfts   e. experience

6. min   f. references
7. ref   g. full-time
8. F/T   h. minimum
9. P/T   i. necessary
10. nec   j. part-time

Draw a line from each abbreviation to the correct meaning.

1 CLERICAL. Type 45 wpm. Work with public. Good sal., bnfts. Alpine Company. 10-2 M-F. 812 Boston St.

2 CLERICAL
MOTOR CREDIT CO.
Min. 2 yrs. exp Finance Co. Excellent bnfts. Contact Jim Clark, 291-6650.

3 Nurse's Aides - Days & PMs. Sunshine Nursing Home. 622 So. Willow Road. F/T. Exp. nec.

4 NURSE'S AIDE
Care for handicapped child. Live-in with good family. Weekends off. Ref. req. Good salary. Call Mrs. Johnson, 461-7253.

Pair Practice: Ask and answer these questions with your teacher. Then ask your partner.

1. Which clerical job requires experience with a finance company?

2. Which nurse's aide job asks you to live in someone's house?

3. Which nurse's aide job asks that you have references?

4. Which clerical job requires you to type 45 wpm?

READING THE WANT ADS

A: Here's an ad for a mechanic.
B: What does it say?
A: It says, *5-day week, salary, paid vacation, benefits.*
B: That's good. You should call right now.

PRACTICE

Here's an ad for a mechanic.
                    tailor.
                    welder.
                    secretary.

It says, *5-day week.*
          $4.50 an hour.
          insurance.
          pension plan.
          benefits.

A PART-TIME JOB

A: Look! Did you see that ad?
B: Yes. *Part-time gardener,
Call Town House Apartments,
563-7851.*
A: That's near where you live.
Why don't you call?
B: I will. I need to earn
some spending money.

PRACTICE

I need to earn some spending money.
          make   extra

Pair Practice: Ask and answer these questions with your teacher and then with your partner.

When you look for a job, do you read the want ads?
Do you read want ads in the newspaper? on bulletin boards?

VOCATIONAL TRAINING

A: I need a job. Do you have training classes here?
B: Yes, we have many job training classes.
A: What kind?
B: Auto body, auto mechanics, upholstery, and. . .
A: How long is the training?
B: Each class is different.

PRACTICE

I need a job.
     training.
     experience.
     skills.

We have auto mechanics training.
     auto body
     upholstery
     dry cleaning

Pair Practice: Look at the pictures. Then ask and answer questions about each picture with your teacher and then with your partner.

EXAMPLE:
1. What training is this?   Welding.
2. Are you interested in it?   Yes, I am.
3. Do you think it is a good job?   Yes, you can make a lot of money.

I'M LOOKING FOR A JOB

A: Hello.
B: I'm calling about the secretary's job.
A: How fast can you type?
B: Forty-five words per minute.
A: OK. Come in and pick up an application, please.

PRACTICE

Can you type?
       take shorthand?
       use a word processor?
       use a computer?

MAKING AN APPOINTMENT

A: Good afternoon.
B: This is Jane Morton. I want to make an appointment for an interview.
A: Did you fill out an application?
B: Yes, I did.
A: Fine. Can you be here tomorrow at 3 P.M.?
B: Yes. I'll be there. Thank you.

PRACTICE

Did you fill out an application?
       complete
       send in

Pair Practice: Ask and answer these questions with your teacher and then with your partner.

Did you ever call about a job?
Did you go for an interview?
What happened?

A JOB INTERVIEW

A: Are you looking for full-time or part-time work?
B: Full-time. What is the pay?
A: It's $4.75 an hour, plus tips. The job is on the late shift.
B: That's fine.
A: I have to interview three more people. I'll let you know next week.

PRACTICE

I am looking for full-time work.   I can work the day shift.
            part-time   night
                                         late

A FOLLOW-UP CALL

A: Hello. This is Susan Brown. I had an interview last week.
   Is the job still open?
B: I'm sorry. Someone else got the job.
A: Oh! Can you tell me why?
B: I'm sorry. I don't know. We may have more
   openings later.

Pair Practice: Ask and answer the following questions with your teacher and then with your partner.

How do you think Susan feels?
Do you think she will apply again?
Why do you think she didn't get the job?
What can she do now?

Pair Practice: Talk about the job applicants in this picture with your teacher and your class. Describe the two women.

What are they wearing?

What are they doing?

Who do you think will get the job?

ASKING ABOUT BENEFITS

A: Do you have any questions?
B: Yes, can you tell me about the benefits?
A: We offer complete health benefits and, after six months, one day a month sick leave.
B: Is there paid vacation?
A: Yes. You get one week after the first year.

_____ Practice A Job Interview

Pair Practice: Ask and answer questions about each job with your teacher and then with your partner.

	SALARY	HOURS	SICK LEAVE	VACATION	HEALTH BENEFITS
Job 1	$180/wk	3-11 P.M.	6 days/year	1 week each yr	yes
Job 2	$800/mo	12-9 P.M.	2 days/mo	2 weeks each yr	yes
Job 3	$4.50/hr	9-6 P.M.	no	no	no

EXAMPLE: Job 1 What is the salary?
What are the hours?
Do I get sick leave? vacation? health benefits?

MY FIRST PAYCHECK!

A: I got my first paycheck today!
B: How much did you make?
A: I made $256, but I only got $206.40.
B: That's because they take out federal and state taxes and Social Security.
A: So many deductions!

PRACTICE

How much did you make?   They take out taxes.
           earn?   deduct
           receive?   withhold
           get?

A Sample Paycheck

Pair Practice: Ask and answer questions about the paycheck with your teacher and then with your partner.

GREEN TOOL COMPANY
"Tools for you since 1922"

Statement of earnings and payroll deductions

Employee no. ___763___   Date ___July 1, 1990___

Total hours	Hourly rate	Regular earnings	Overtime earnings	Gross earnings	Federal tax	State tax	FICA	Total deduc.
40	6.40/hr	256.00	—	256.00	25.60	6.00	18.00	49.60

Period ending ___6/3/90___   NET PAY ___$206.40___

EXAMPLE: How many hours did the employee work?
How. What is the hourly rate?

Pair Practice: Practice with your teacher first and then with your partner. Student A asks student B for the information missing from part A. Student B asks student A for the information missing from part B.

A

GREEN TOOL COMPANY
"Tools for you since 1922"

Statement of earnings
and payroll deductions

Employee no. ___1963___   Date _____?_____

Total hours	Hourly rate	Regular earnings	Overtime earnings	Gross earnings	Federal tax	State tax	FICA	Total deduc.
?	5.80/hr	?	?	290.00	25.00	?	22.00	55.00

Period ending _____8/31/90_____   NET PAY _____?_____

B

GREEN TOOL COMPANY
"Tools for you since 1922"

Statement of earnings
and payroll deductions

Employee no. ____?____   Date ___September 10, 1990___

Total hours	Hourly rate	Regular earnings	Overtime earnings	Gross earnings	Federal tax	State tax	FICA	Total deduc.
40	?	232.00	58.00	290.00	?	8.00	?	?

Period ending _____?_____   NET PAY ___$235.00___

EXAMPLE: A: How many hours did the employee work?
          B: Forty hours. What's the hourly rate?
          A: It's $5.80.

JOB REVIEW

A: Good afternoon.
B: Good afternoon, Tom. Is this your first job review?
A: Yes.
B: Your work is good, but you were late four times last month.
A: I know. I used to ride the bus. I have a car now.
B: OK. You'll get a raise next month if you are on time.
A: OK. Thank you.

PRACTICE

Your work is good.
    satisfactory.
    slow.

Pair Practice: Ask and answer these questions with your teacher and your class. Then ask your partner.

Was this a good review? Why? Why not?
Do you think he will get a raise later?
Do you have job reviews at work?

FILLING OUT A JOB APPLICATION

Lisa Hess is looking for a job. Use the following information to fill out the application.

Lisa is married. She lives at 1047 Cameron Street in Miami, Florida, 86201. Her telephone number is (305) 742-6311. She is applying for a secretary's job. She will bring a birth certificate to prove that she is a U.S. citizen. Her Social Security number is 759-43-2160. She graduated from high school five years ago. She worked three years as a secretary. She worked for Red River Auto Parts for $6.50 an hour from June 1983 to August 1986. Her boss was Tom Root. The company's address is 13795 First Street, Miami, Florida. Mr. Root's telephone number is 647-9326.

JOB APPLICATION

1. Job applying for _____

2. Name
   Mr.
   Mrs. _____
   Miss (Print)   Last   First   Middle

3. Address _____
   Number and street

   _____ 4. Telephone ( ) _____
   City   State   Zip code

5. ___ - ___ - ___   6. U.S.   ☐ yes   7. Do you have a   ☐ yes
   Social Security number   citizen ☐ no   legal right to   ☐ no
                                                    work in the U.S.?

8. Marital status: Single ☐ Married ☐ Widowed ☐ Divorced ☐

9. Do you have a high school diploma? yes ☐   no ☐

10. List your job experience:

From mo/yr	To mo/yr	Employer's name, address, and telephone	Salary	Position

Signature _____   Date _____

Fill out this application with information about yourself.

JOB APPLICATION

1. Job applying for _____

2. Name
   Mr.
   Mrs.
   Miss _____
   (Print) Last   First   Middle

3. Address _____
   Number and street

   _____ 4. Telephone (   ) _____
   City   State   Zip code

5. _____   6. U.S.   ☐ yes   7. Do you have a   ☐ yes
   - Social Security number   citizen   ☐ no   legal right to   ☐ no
                                                     work in the U.S.?

8. Marital status: Single ☐ Married ☐ Widowed ☐ Divorced ☐

9. Do you have a high school diploma? yes ☐   no ☐

10. List your job experience:

From mo/yr	To mo/yr	Employer's name, address, and telephone	Salary	Position

Signature _____   Date _____

LOOKING FOR A JOB

Susan Tom needs a job. She wants to be a word processor. She reads the ads in the newspaper. She finds an ad and calls for an interview. During the interviews the interviewer asks her many questions about her experience. She asks the interviewer questions about the job and benefits. She wants to work full-time. The salary is $7.50 an hour. The hours are from 9 A.M. to 5 P.M. She hopes she gets the job.

QUESTIONS

1. What kind of work is Susan Tom looking for?
2. What does the interviewer ask about?
3. What does Susan ask about?

YES/NO

Read each sentence. Circle yes or no after each sentence.

1. Susan wants to be a police officer.   Yes   (No)
2. She reads the ads in the newspaper.   Yes   No
3. Susan wants to work part-time.   Yes   No
4. The job is on the night shift.   Yes   No

WRITE ABOUT YOURSELF

1. Do you work? _____

   _____

2. What is your occupation? _____

   _____

3. Did you work in your country? _____

   _____

4. What kind of work did you do? _____

   _____

5. What kind of job do you want in the United States? _____

   _____

chapter **8**

BANKING AND MONEY ORDERS

COMPETENCY OBJECTIVES

On completion of this chapter, the students will show orally, in writing, or through demonstration that they are able to use language needed in the following situations:

A. BANKING

- Provide personal information.
- Differentiate between checking and savings accounts.
- Make a deposit.
- Fill out and cash a personal check.

B. MONEY ORDERS

- Buy a money order at a bank.
- Identify other locations where money orders can be purchased.
- Fill out a money order.

I NEED SOME INFORMATION

A: I'd like to open an account.
B: I need some information first.
   What's your name?
A: John R. Smith.
B: What's your address?
A: 9078 West Hemp Street,
   San Diego, California 92113.
B: What's your Social Security number?
A: 278–89–0021.
B: What's your mother's maiden name?
A: Johnson.
B: Thank you.

Pair Practice: Ask and answer these questions with your teacher. Then ask your partner. Write the information your partner tells you on the form below.

What is your name?
What is your address?
What is your Social Security number?
What is your mother's maiden name?

NAME _____

ADDRESS _____

SOCIAL SECURITY _____

MOTHER'S MAIDEN NAME _____

Pair Practice: Talk about the picture with your teacher and then with your partner. Then read each of the following sentences. Your partner writes the number of the sentence on the blank line next to the correct picture.

EXAMPLE: A: (Reads sentence 1.) The name of the bank is First Bank.
B: (Finds the correct picture and writes *1* on the blank line next to the name of the bank.)

A

1. The name of the bank is First Bank.
3. She's making a deposit at the counter.
5. He's waiting in line to withdraw money.

B

2. She's opening a new account.
4. They want to borrow money. They want a loan.
5. The teller window is closed.

CHECKING OR SAVINGS?

A: I'd like to open an account, please.
B: Checking or savings?
A: What's the difference?
B: In a checking account, you deposit money and write checks.
A: I see . . .and a savings account?
B: You deposit money and leave it there to earn interest. You withdraw it when you need it.

PRACTICE

You deposit money.
   put in
   withdraw
   take out

You withdraw money for an emergency.
         when you need it.

Pair Practice: Ask and answer these questions with your teacher. Then ask your partner.

1. Do you think banks are a good place to put your money? Why? Why not?
2. Do you have a bank account? If yes, what kind?
3. Did you have a bank account in your country?
4. How do most people pay their bills in your country?

THE MINIMUM DEPOSIT IS $100

A: How much would you like to deposit in your new account today?
B: What is the minimum deposit?
A: It's $100.
B: I'll deposit $150.
A: Fine. Here are your temporary checks. Your personalized checks will come in the mail.

PRACTICE

How much would you like to deposit?
How much should I   deposit?
                put in?

The minimum is $100.
            $500.
            $1,000.

Your personalized checks will come in the
                          mail.
                          be sent.
                          delivered.

Pair Practice: Ask and answer questions about the check with your teacher. Then ask your partner.

JOHN R. SMITH
ROSE A. SMITH
736 Pine St. 492-7770
San Diego, Calif. 92110

206

Dec. 6 19 90   90-59 / 1222

PAY TO THE
ORDER OF *Bill Johnson* $31 27/XXX

Thirty-one and 27/00   DOLLARS

FIRST WORLD BANK
2200 Main Street
San Diego, Calif. 92111

Rose Smith

MEMO

⑆1222⑈0059⑆0041311531⑈ 0206

EXAMPLE:
1. What is the name of the bank?
2. How much is the check for?
3. What is the date on the check?
4. Who is the check for?
5. Who wrote the check?

I WANT TO CASH THIS CHECK

A: May I help you?
B: Yes, I want to cash this check.
A: Do you have ID?
B: Yes, I do.
A: OK. Please endorse your check on the back.
B: I'm sorry. I don't understand you.
A: Sign your name on the back.

Do You Have ID?

Pair Practice: Practice the following conversations with your teacher and then with your partner. Substitute the numbered words in the boxes for the underlined words in the conversation.

1. money order	1. paycheck	1. welfare check
2. a driver's license	2. identification	2. ID
3. Yes.	3. No.	3. Yes.
4. Sign on the back, please.	4. I'm sorry, we can't cash it then.	4. Sign here, please.

EXAMPLE: A: I want to cash this <u>money order</u> .
                              1

                B: Do you have <u>a driver's license</u> ?
                                     2

                A: <u>Yes</u> .
                      3

                B: <u>Sign on the back</u> .
                          4

WHERE CAN I BUY A MONEY ORDER? _____

A: I need to buy a money order. Where can I get one?
B: You can buy a money order at the post office or a bank.
A: OK. Are there any other places?
B: Sure. At the supermarket or the check cashing service.

PRACTICE

Where can I buy one?   You can buy one at the store or bank.
    get   get   bank   post office.
    purchase   purchase

Pair Practice: Ask and answer these questions with your teacher. Then ask your partner.

EXAMPLE: 1.   Do you ever buy money orders?
                2.   Where do you buy them?
                3.   What do you buy them for?

I'D LIKE TO BUY A MONEY ORDER

A: May I help you?
B: Yes. I'd like to buy a money order.
A: For how much?
B: For $80.
A: Fill out the amount and sign your name. The total is $81.
B: $81?
A: Yes, $80 for the money order and a $1 service fee.

Fill out the money order below. Use the following information:

Date: September 27, 1990
Pay to: Walton's Department Store

Bank of USA
MONEY ORDER

DATE_____19___

PAY TO _____

AMOUNT _____ *-Eighty Dollars -*_____$_____

Signature_____Address_____

003479:167290-0902

Maria wants to open a checking account. With a checking account, she can deposit money and write checks to pay bills. In her bank, the minimum deposit is $100. Maria will receive personalized checks to use. Today, Maria received her paycheck from work. It was for $235.57. She deposited her paycheck in her new checking account.

QUESTIONS

1. What kind of account did Maria want?
2. What is the minimum deposit?
3. How much did Maria receive in her paycheck?

YES/NO

Read each sentence. Circle yes or no after each sentence.

1.	Maria wants to open a savings account.	(Yes)	No
2.	Maria will receive personalized checks to use.	Yes	No
3.	Maria received her welfare check.	Yes	No
4.	She earned $235.57.	Yes	No

WRITE ABOUT YOURSELF

1. Do you have a checking account? _____

   _____

2. Do you have a savings account? _____

   _____

3. What can you use a savings account for? _____

   _____

chapter  9

COMMUNITY RESOURCES

COMPETENCY OBJECTIVES

On completion of this chapter, the students will show orally, in writing, or through demonstration that they are able to use language needed in the following situations:

A. POST OFFICE

- Buy stamps.
- Mail a package or a letter.
- Insure or register mail.
- Fill out a change-of-address form.

B. ADULT SCHOOLS AND DAYCARE CENTERS

- Locate and register in adult classes.
- Locate and register children in daycare centers.

C. PUBLIC HEALTH AND OTHER COMMUNITY AGENCIES

- Identify agencies and describe their services.

D. PUBLIC LIBRARY

- Locate and use library services.

FIVE 25¢ STAMPS, PLEASE

A: Next person in line.
B: I'd like to buy five 25¢ stamps, please.
A: Excuse me, what did you say?
B: Five 25¢ stamps.
A: Oh, here you are, that's $1.25.

PRACTICE

I'd like to buy stamps.
              an aerogramme.
              an envelope.
              a box.
              a money order.

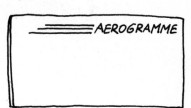

Pair Practice: Ask and answer these questions with your teacher. Then ask your partner.

1. Do you go to the post office? What do you go there for?
2. Where is the post office nearest to your house?
3. How often do you go to the post office?
4. What do you buy there?

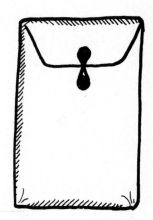

	A	B	C
1.	15 50¢	50 15¢	50 50¢
2.	5 25¢	25 5¢	5 20¢
3.	10 1¢	1 10¢	10 10¢
4.	10 25¢	11 25¢	25 10¢
5.	15 1¢	1 15¢	50 1¢
6.	13 3¢	30 3¢	33 3¢
7.	2 20¢	2 22¢	20 2¢
8.	5 5 ¢	5 1¢	1 15¢

Listen to your teacher and circle the numbers that he or she says.

EXAMPLE: Teacher: I want to buy 15 50¢ stamps.
Students circle: 15 - 50¢

Pair Practice: Talk about the picture with your teacher and then with your partner. Then read each of the following sentences. Your partner writes the number of the sentence on the blank line next to the correct picture.

EXAMPLE: A: (Reads sentence 1.) He is mailing a package.
             B: (Finds the correct picture and writes *1* on the blank line next to the man at the counter.)

A
1. He is mailing a package.
3. They are playing on the floor.
5. He is opening his post office box.
7. They are filling out forms.

B
2. It's 11:00 o'clock.
4. She is buying an aerogram.
6. She is mailing a letter.

INSURED MAIL

A: I'd like to insure this package.
B: What's in it?
A: A watch.
B: How much is it worth?
A: $175.
B: Where is it going?
A: To New York.
B: OK. The insurance is $2.25, and the postage is $1.65 for first class. You need to fill out this form for the insurance.

Sender fills out this form

Post clerk fills out this form

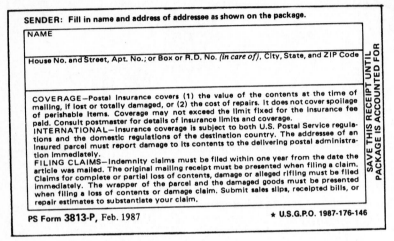

SENDER: Fill in name and address of addressee as shown on the package.

NAME

House No. and Street, Apt. No.; or Box or R.D. No. *(in care of)*, City, State, and ZIP Code

COVERAGE—Postal insurance covers (1) the value of the contents at the time of mailing, if lost or totally damaged, or (2) the cost of repairs. It does not cover spoilage of perishable items. Coverage may not exceed the limit fixed for the insurance fee paid. Consult postmaster for details of insurance limits and coverage.
INTERNATIONAL—Insurance coverage is subject to both U.S. Postal Service regulations and the domestic regulations of the destination country. The addressee of an insured parcel must report damage to its contents to the delivering postal administration immediately.
FILING CLAIMS—Indemnity claims must be filed within one year from the date the article was mailed. The original mailing receipt must be presented when filing a claim. Claims for complete or partial loss of contents, damage or alleged rifling must be filed immediately. The wrapper of the parcel and the damaged goods must be presented when filing a loss of contents or damage claim. Submit sales slips, receipted bills, or repair estimates to substantiate your claim.

PS Form **3813-P**, Feb. 1987   ★ U.S.G.P.O. 1987-176-146

SAVE THIS RECEIPT UNTIL PACKAGE IS ACCOUNTED FOR

V—345 487 275

RECEIPT FOR INSURED MAIL
DOMESTIC—INTERNATIONAL

ADDRESSED FOR DELIVERY AT
(Post Office, State and Country)

#18   New York

| POSTAGE | AIR | $ 1.65 |

INSURANCE COVERAGE   FEE

$ 175.00 $ 2.25

SPECIAL HANDLING	$
DOMES-TIC ONLY ▶ Special Delivery	$
▶ Restricted Delivery	$

RETURN RECEIPT
(Except to Canada)   ¢

Fragile Liquid Perishable   TOTAL
☐   ☐   ☐ $ 3.90

(Postmark)   Customer Over ▶

Postmaster By *HL*

U.S. MAIL INSURED

V—345 487 275

NOTE: To file claim for damage or loss of contents, you must present the article, container and packaging.

Pair Practice: Ask and answer these questions with your teacher. Then ask your partner.

1. Did you ever insure a package?
2. What was in it?
3. How much was the insurance?
4. Did the package arrive safely?
5. What should you do if there is a problem with an insured package?

REGISTERED OR CERTIFIED MAIL?

A: I want to mail this letter. It's very important.
   I want to make sure it gets there.
B: You can send it by certified mail.
A: What's certified mail?
B: When certified mail is delivered, someone
   at the address signs a receipt card, and then you
   get the card back.
A: OK. I'll send it certified.

PRACTICE

I want to make sure it gets there.
         be certain
         sure

I'll send it certified.
    mail   registered.
           insured.

SENDER: Complete items 1 and 2 when additional services are desired, and complete items 3 and 4.
Put your address in the "RETURN TO" Space on the reverse side. Failure to do this will prevent this card from being returned to you. The return receipt fee will provide you the name of the person delivered to and the date of delivery. For additional fees the following services are available. Consult postmaster for fees and check box(es) for additional service(s) requested.
1. ☐ Show to whom delivered, date, and addressee's address.   2. ☐ Restricted Delivery
     (Extra charge)   *(Extra charge)*

3. Article Addressed to:

4. Article Number

Type of Service:
☐ Registered   ☐ Insured
☐ Certified   ☐ COD
☐ Express Mail   ☐ Return Receipt
                     for Merchandise

Always obtain signature of addressee
or agent and DATE DELIVERED.

5. Signature — Address
X

6. Signature — Agent
X

7. Date of Delivery

8. Addressee's Address *(ONLY if requested and fee paid)*

PS Form **3811,** Mar. 1988   ★ U.S.G.P.O. 1988-212-865   **DOMESTIC RETURN RECEIPT**

Pair Practice: Ask and answer these questions about the receipt card with your teacher.
Then ask your partner. Write the answers in the space provided.

1. On which line do you sign your name?   _____

2. On which line does the postal worker sign?   _____

3. On which line is the address for the receiver?   _____

4. On which line is the delivery date?   _____

5. On which line is the article number?   _____

THE MOSS FAMILY MOVES

The Moss family is moving. They want to be sure that mail comes to their new house. There are four people in the Moss family: Mr. Bob Moss, Mrs. Jan Moss, David Moss, and Rick Moss. Their old address is: 2775 Tate St. #30 San Diego, CA 92115. Their new address is: 437 Main St. El Cajon, CA 92077. They are moving on October 1, 1990

Change of Address Order

Pair Practice: Work with your partner. Fill out the Change of Address Order for the Moss family.

U.S. Postal Service **CHANGE OF ADDRESS ORDER**	Customer Instructions: Complete Items 1 thru 9. Except Item 8, please PRINT all information including address on face of card.	**OFFICIAL USE ONLY**

1. Change of Address for *(Check one)* ☐ Individual ☐ Entire Family ☐ Business

Zone/Route ID No.

2. Start Date — Month Day Year

3. If TEMPORARY address, print date to discontinue forwarding — Month Day Year

Date Entered on Form 3982
M M D D Y Y

4. Print Last Name or Name of Business *(If more than one, use separate Change of Address Order Form for each)*

Expiration Date
M M D D Y Y

5. Print First Name of Head of Household *(include Jr., Sr., etc.).* Leave blank if the Change of Address Order is for a business.

Clerk/Carrier Endorsement

6. Print **OLD** mailing address, number and street *(if Puerto Rico, include urbanization zone)*

Apt./Suite No.   P.O. Box No.   R.R/HCR No.   Rural Box/HCR Box No.

City   State   ZIP Code

7. Print **NEW** mailing address, number and street *(if Puerto Rico, include urbanization zone)*

Apt./Suite No.   P.O. Box No.   R.R/HCR No.   Rural Box/HCR Box No.

City   State   ZIP Code

8. Signature *(See conditions on reverse)*

OFFICIAL USE ONLY

9. Date Signed — Month Day Year

OFFICIAL USE ONLY

Verification Endorsement

PS Form 3575, Mar. 1988

★USGPO-1988-210-546

READING EXERCISE

When Mrs. Park is out of stamps, she goes to the post office. If she needs a money order, she can buy it there, too. Sometimes she has something important to mail. If she wants to make sure it is received, she sends it by certified mail. If it is something very expensive, she insures it. It costs a little more money, but it's the safest way.

QUESTIONS

1. Where does Mrs. Park go to buy stamps?
2. How does she send important mail?
3. How does she send something expensive?

YES/NO

Read each sentence. Circle *yes* or *no* after each sentence.

1. When Mrs. Park is out of stamps, she goes to the department store.   Yes   (No)
2. If she has something important to send, she sends it by certified mail.   Yes   No
3. If it is something expensive, she insures it.   Yes   No
4. She can buy a money order at the post office.   Yes   No

WRITE ABOUT YOURSELF

1. Do you send letters? _____

   _____

2. What do you buy at the post office? _____

   _____

3. Do you ever send certified mail? _____

   _____

4. Do you ever send insured mail? _____

   _____

5. Do you ever send registered mail? _____

   _____

I NEED SOME INFORMATION, PLEASE

A: Hi. I need some information about classes here.
B: What can I help you with?
A: Do you have sewing classes?
B: Yes. Mondays and Wednesdays.
A: What time?
B: From 3 to 6 P.M.
A: How do I register?
B: Just go to the class. It's in room 17.

PRACTICE

Do you have sewing classes here?
    typing
    English
    auto mechanics
    electronic assembly
    cooking

How do I register?
    enroll?

Pair Practice: Ask and answer these questions with your teacher. Then ask your partner.

1. What school do you go to?
2. What class do you go to?
3. What days and times do you go to class?
4. What other classes would you like to take?

ADULT SCHOOL

CLASS	DAYS	TIME	ROOM	INSTRUCTOR
ART				
Art History	W	8-10am	15	Smith
Painting	Th	8-10am	15	Smith
BUSINESS				
Typing	Th,F	3-5pm	26	Martin
Computer	M,W,F	3-5pm	27	Babbit
Accounting	T,Th	8-10am	20	McKee
ENGLISH AS A SECOND LANGUAGE				
Beginning	M-F	9-12noon	33	Garvey
Intermediate	M-F	9-12noon	34	Chang
Advanced	M-F	9-12noon	35	Howard
HOME ECONOMICS				
Sewing Basics	M,W	9-12pm	17	Jones
Cooking	T,Th	1-4pm	5	Nelley
VOCATIONAL ED				
Auto Mechanics	M-F	8-3:30pm	2	Benson
Electronic Assembly	M-F	8-3:30pm	4	Shoop

Work with your partner. Use the schedule above to fill out the chart.

		Time	Days	Instructor
1.	Sewing class	_____	_____	_____
2.	Typing class	_____	_____	_____
3.	Auto mechanics	_____	_____	_____
4.	Beginning English	_____	_____	_____
5.	Cooking class	_____	_____	_____
6.	Electronics Assembly	_____	_____	_____
7.	Computer class	_____	_____	_____
8.	Intermediate English	_____	_____	_____
9.	Painting	_____	_____	_____
10.	Accounting	_____	_____	_____

PUBLIC HEALTH SERVICES

A: I have to register my son for kindergarten.
B: Do you have his birth certificate and immunization record?
A: I have the birth certificate, but he needs shots.
B: You can get free shots at the Public Health Department. Be sure to call before you go.

PRACTICE

I have to register my son for kindergarten.
                                    preschool.
                                    elementary school.
                                    junior high school.
                                    high school.

Do you have his immunization records?
                    vaccination
                    shot
                    health

He needs a smallpox immunization.
            polio
            TB
            mumps

Pair Practice: Ask and answer these questions with your teacher. Then ask your partner.

1. If you have children, do you have immunization records for them?
2. Do you have immunization records for yourself?
3. Do you go to the Public Health Department?
4. If you have children, did you get shots for them and yourself in your country?

WHERE IS YOUR CLINIC?

A: Hello, Public Health. Can I help you?
B: Yes. I live on Tate Street. Where is your nearest office?
A: At the corner of 51st and Main streets.
B: What days do you give DPT shots?
A: Mondays and Wednesdays from 1 P.M. to 4 P.M.

PRACTICE

Where is your office?   At the corner of B Street and 10th.
      are you located?   On B Street.
      can I find your office?   Between A Street and B Street on 10th.

Pair Practice: Ask and answer these questions with your teacher. Then ask your partner.

1. Do you know where the Public Health Department is?
2. Is there a clinic near your house?
3. How can the Public Health Clinic help you?
4. Where do you go for shots?

Write the address and telephone number of the Public Health Clinic in your area.

Address _____ Phone _____

Pair Practice: Ask and answer these questions with your teacher. Then ask your partner. Use the information below to fill in the blanks.

AUTOMOBILES		
Department of Motor Vehicles	Info	757-3233
	Licenses	757-3200
EDUCATION—ADULT SCHOOL		457-6839
EMPLOYMENT		
Employment Development Department	Info	650-1000
HEALTH		
Public Health Department	Info	757-4100
LEGAL		
Legal Aid	1-800-842-8437	
LIBRARIES		948-3681
POLICE AND FIRE DEPARTMENTS	Emergency Only 911	
POST OFFICE	Info	347-8924
RECREATION CENTER		973-6913
SOCIAL SECURITY OFFICE		980-8009
DEPARTMENT OF SOCIAL SERVICES	Info	563-9440
Food Stamps		963-6275

EXAMPLE: A: My son needs shots. Who do I call?
          B: Call the Public Health Department, 757-4100.

1. My son needs shots. Who do I call? _____

2. I need to renew my driver's license. Who do I call? _____

    _____

3. I have problems with my landlord. Who do I call? _____

    _____

4. I need to apply for a Social Security card. Who do I call? _____

    _____

5. I need help looking for a job. Who do I call? _____

    _____

6. I want to know where my children can learn to play tennis. Who do I call?

    _____

DAYCARE CENTERS

> A: I must get a job. But first I have to go back to school to learn more English.
>
> B: What are you going to do with the children?
>
> A: Well, Joe is in first grade now. And I'm going to put Sara into a daycare center.
>
> B: Good idea. Is it expensive?
>
> A: No, we pay according to our income. I hope there is no waiting list.

PRACTICE

I must get a job.
  need to

I have to learn English.
       earn money.
       get a job.
       go back to school.
       find a daycare center.

We pay according to our income.
                 ability.
      only what we can afford.
We pay what we can.

Pair Practice: Ask and answer these questions with your teacher. Then ask your partner.

1. Do you have children? How many?
2. How old are your children?
3. Do you take your children to daycare?
4. Is it free?
5. Is it near your house? work? school?

TYKUS DAYCARE CENTER _____

A: Hello, Tykus Daycare Center.
B: Hello, I need some information. Do you have any openings?
A: Yes, we do.
B: What are the rates?
A: It depends on your income. Please come in and talk to us.

TYKUS DAYCARE CENTER
3175 West Gate Road   475-3369

DAYS	TIME
Monday–Friday	6 A.M.–7 P.M.
Saturday	8 A.M.–5 P.M.

AGE	COST	
2 mos.–1 yr.	$80 wk.	$300 mo.
1 yr.–6 yrs.	$60 wk.	$200 mo.

Lower rates available on proof of monthly income

STATE LICENSED

Pair Practice: Ask and answer these questions with your teacher and then with your partner.

1. Where is the Tykus Daycare Center?
2. What is the telephone number?
3. What days is the daycare center open?
4. How much is monthly daycare for an 11-month-old baby?
5. How much is weekly care for a five-year-old?
6. Does the daycare center have a license?
7. What do you think a license for daycare is?

Pair Practice: Talk about the picture with your teacher and then with your partner. Then read each of the following sentences. Your partner writes the number of the sentence on the blank line next to the correct picture.

EXAMPLE:　A:　(Reads sentence 1.) The little boy is reading a book.
　　　　　　B:　(Finds the correct picture and writes *1* on the blank line next to the little boy reading a book.)

1. The little boy is reading a book.
2. She is listening to a tape.
3. He is checking out a book.
4. He is looking at new books.
5. She is returning books.

I'D LIKE TO GET A LIBRARY CARD

A: I'd like to get a library card.
B: Can I see your driver's license?
A: I don't have one. But I do have an ID card.
B: All right. You need to show me a piece of mail with your address on it.
A: Can I bring it tomorrow?
B: Sure. See you tomorrow.

Pair Practice: Ask and answer these questions with your teacher. Then ask your partner.

1. Do you have a library card?
2. Do you go to the library?
3. What do you get at the library?
4. Is there a library near your house?

_____ **USING COMMUNITY RESOURCES**

When parents go to work or school, they can take their children to daycare centers. Of course, when the children are older, they go to school. Before parents can register children for kindergarten they have to have their children's birth certificates and immunization records. Parents can take their children to the public health clinic for free immunization and TB tests. They can call the health department to find the clinic nearest to them.

QUESTIONS

1. When parents work, where can they take their small children?
2. What must parents have before they register their children for kindergarten?
3. Where can people go for free immunization shots?

YES/NO

Read each sentence. Circle yes or no after each sentence.

1. Parents can take their children to daycare centers.   (Yes)   No
2. The children can get free shots at the daycare center.   Yes   No
3. People can get free shots at the public health center.   Yes   No
4. Parents must have their children's birth certificates and immunization records before they can register their children for kindergarten.   Yes   No

WRITE ABOUT YOURSELF

1. Do you have small children? How many? _____

   _____

2. Do they go to a childcare center? Where? _____

   _____

3. Is there a public health clinic near your house? _____

   _____

chapter 10

UNITED STATES HISTORICAL HOLIDAYS

COMPETENCY OBJECTIVES

On completion of this chapter, the students will show orally, in writing, or through demonstration that they are able to use language needed in the following situations:

A. LOCATE THE DATES OF MAJOR U.S. HISTORICAL HOLIDAYS ON A CALENDAR.

- Martin Luther King, Jr.; January 15
- Abraham Lincoln; February 12
- George Washington; February 22
- Memorial Day; May 30, or last Monday in May
- Independence Day; July 4
- Columbus Day; October 12
- Thanksgiving Day; fourth Thursday in November

B. STATE THE NAMES OF MAJOR U.S. HISTORICAL HOLIDAYS.

C. TELL ABOUT A PERSON OR EVENT RELATED TO MAJOR U.S. HISTORICAL HOLIDAYS.

HOLIDAYS

All countries celebrate special days, called holidays. Many holidays help people remember times in history or famous people. Many holidays are the same around the world.

Do you celebrate Independence Day in your country? Do you have a holiday to give thanks? What other important holidays do you have in your country? What are the dates?

Circle the following dates on the calendars below:

January 15
February 12
February 15; third Monday in February
February 22
May 24; fourth Monday in May
July 4
October 12
November 26; fourth Thursday in November

JANUARY

S	M	T	W	Th	F	S
					1	2
3	4	5	6	7	8	9
10	11	12	13	14	15	16
17	18	19	20	21	22	23
24 31	25	26	27	28	29	30

FEBRUARY

S	M	T	W	Th	F	S
	1	2	3	4	5	6
7	8	9	10	11	12	13
14	15	16	17	18	19	20
21	22	23	24	25	26	27
28						

MARCH

S	M	T	W	Th	F	S
	1	2	3	4	5	6
7	8	9	10	11	12	13
14	15	16	17	18	19	20
21	22	23	24	25	26	27
28	29	30	31			

APRIL

S	M	T	W	Th	F	S
				1	2	3
4	5	6	7	8	9	10
11	12	13	14	15	16	17
18	19	20	21	22	23	24
25	26	27	28	29	30	

MAY

S	M	T	W	Th	F	S
						1
2	3	4	5	6	7	8
9	10	11	12	13	14	15
16	17	18	19	20	21	22
23 30	24 31	25	26	27	28	29

JUNE

S	M	T	W	Th	F	S
		1	2	3	4	5
6	7	8	9	10	11	12
13	14	15	16	17	18	19
20	21	22	23	24	25	26
27	28	29	30			

JULY

S	M	T	W	Th	F	S
				1	2	3
4	5	6	7	8	9	10
11	12	13	14	15	16	17
18	19	20	21	22	23	24
25	26	27	28	29	30	31

AUGUST

S	M	T	W	Th	F	S
1	2	3	4	5	6	7
8	9	10	11	12	13	14
15	16	17	18	19	20	21
22	23	24	25	26	27	28
29	30	31				

SEPTEMBER

S	M	T	W	Th	F	S
			1	2	3	4
5	6	7	8	9	10	11
12	13	14	15	16	17	18
19	20	21	22	23	24	25
26	27	28	29	30		

OCTOBER

S	M	T	W	Th	F	S
					1	2
3	4	5	6	7	8	9
10	11	12	13	14	15	16
17	18	19	20	21	22	23
24 31	25	26	27	28	29	30

NOVEMBER

S	M	T	W	Th	F	S
	1	2	3	4	5	6
7	8	9	10	11	12	13
14	15	16	17	18	19	20
21	22	23	24	25	26	27
28	29	30				

DECEMBER

S	M	T	W	Th	F	S
			1	2	3	4
5	6	7	8	9	10	11
12	13	14	15	16	17	18
19	20	21	22	23	24	25
26	27	28	29	30	31	

MARTIN LUTHER KING DAY: JANUARY 15 _____

BEFORE YOU READ:

Do you know these words?　　laws　　　　　protest　　　　equal
　　　　　　　　　　　　　　birthday　　　　shot
　　　　　　　　　　　　　　minister　　　　march
　　　　　　　　　　　　　　civil rights

　　Look at a calendar for this year. What day is January 15?
　　Do you think all people have equal rights in the United States?
　　Do you think all people have equal rights in your country?

TALK WITH YOUR TEACHER

　　Who was Martin Luther King, Jr.?
　　How did Martin Luther King, Jr. help gain equal rights for all Americans?
　　How did Martin Luther King, Jr. die?

MARTIN LUTHER KING _____

Dr. Martin Luther King, Jr. was born on January 15, 1929. On his birthday, people remember this famous American. Dr. King was a minister. He lived in the South. He did not think the laws were equal for all people. He wanted to change the laws.

In 1963, 250,000 people marched with him in Washington D.C. They wanted to change the laws, too. This was a civil rights march. Some laws were changed after many civil rights protests. More people voted. Schools were open to everyone. More jobs were open to everyone.

Dr. King was shot and killed in 1968 because some people were angry about the new laws. Today, more people have equal rights because of Martin Luther King, Jr.

YES/NO

Read the article above. Circle *yes* or *no* after each sentence.

1. January 15 is Dr. King's birthday.   (Yes) No
2. Dr. Martin Luther King, Jr. was a minister.   Yes No
3. Dr. King thought the laws were equal for everyone.   Yes No
4. Dr. King was from New York.   Yes No
5. Dr. King marched with 250,000 people to change the laws.   Yes No
6. The right to vote is a civil right.   Yes No

PRESIDENTS' DAY

Abraham Lincoln: February 12
George Washington: February 22
Presidents' Day: Third Monday in February

BEFORE YOU READ:

Do you know these words?

Revolutionary War
independence
Civil War
North
South

lasted
fought
killed

Look at a calendar for this year. When is Presidents' Day this year?
Do you have a president in your country? a king?
Do you have a holiday for a leader of your country?

TALK WITH YOUR TEACHER

Who is the president of the United States now?
Who was George Washington?
Who was Abraham Lincoln?

PRESIDENTS' DAY

Presidents' Day is the third Monday in February. Two American presidents have birthdays in February. Abraham Lincoln's birthday is February 12. George Washington's birthday is February 22. Presidents' Day is between February 12 and February 22.

George Washington was a general during the Revolutionary War. In this war, Americans fought for independence from England. After the war, this country's government was separate from England. George Washington was the first president of the new country from 1789 to 1797. He is called *the father of our country*.

Abraham Lincoln was the sixteenth president of the United States from 1861 to 1865. He was president during the Civil War. The southern states wanted to separate from the northern states. The army of the northern states fought the army of the southern states. The North won the war, and the United States stayed a united country. President Lincoln was shot and killed because he wanted the states to remain one country.

YES/NO

Read the article above. Circle *yes* or *no* after each sentence.

1. Abraham Lincoln was the first president of the United States.   Yes (No)
2. George Washington's birthday is February 22.   Yes   No
3. We remember two presidents on Presidents' Day.   Yes   No
4. Abraham Lincoln is called *the father of our country*.   Yes   No
5. The North and the South fought in the Civil War.   Yes   No
6. The South won the Civil War.   Yes   No

MEMORIAL DAY: LAST MONDAY IN MAY _____

BEFORE YOU READ

Do you know these words?   service men   died
                                     service women   decorate
                                     wreaths   celebrated
                                     graves

Look at a calendar for this year. When is Memorial Day?
Is every holiday a happy time?
In your country, do you have a holiday to honor people who died in war?

TALK WITH YOUR TEACHER

What do service men do? What do service women do?
How do Americans honor service men and women who have died in war?

MEMORIAL DAY

The first Memorial Day was celebrated after the Civil War. Memorial Day is the last Monday in May. On Memorial Day, Americans remember all the service men and women who were killed in war. Service men and women have died in many wars.

In many states, on Memorial Day people remember all of their friends and family who have died. They decorate their graves with flowers and wreaths. Sometimes, Memorial Day is called Decoration Day. Memorial Day is a sad holiday.

YES/NO

Read the article above. Circle *yes* or *no* after each sentence.

1. Memorial Day is in November.   Yes (No)
2. Memorial Day is a happy holiday.   Yes No
3. The first Memorial Day was after the Civil War.   Yes No
4. On Memorial Day we honor service men and women.   Yes No
5. Memorial Day is May first.   Yes No
6. Another name for Memorial Day is Decoration Day.   Yes No

INDEPENDENCE DAY: JULY 4 _____

BEFORE YOU READ

Do you know these words?   government   free
                                           flag   independent
                                           stars   separate
                                         stripes

Look at a calendar for this year. What day is July 4?
Do you have an Independence Day in your country?
What is the date?
Tell about your country's flag.

TALK WITH YOUR TEACHER

What does *independence* mean?
When was the first Independence Day in the United States?
What are the colors of the American flag?
Why does the American flag have 13 stripes?

INDEPENDENCE DAY _____

July 4 is the birthday of the United States of America. On July 4, 1776, the Declaration of Independence was signed. The people in America wanted to be free and independent from England. They wanted a new country and a new government. George Washington was their first president.

You see many flags on Independence Day. The American flag is red, white, and blue. It has 13 red and white stripes. They are for the first 13 states. The first American flag had 13 stars, one star for each state. Now there are 50 stars because there are 50 states. Many people fly the flag on the fourth of July, Independence Day.

YES/NO

Read the article above. Circle *yes* or *no* after each sentence.

1. The Declaration of Independence was signed in 1776.   (Yes) No
2. This country wanted to be separate from England.   Yes   No
3. The first flag had 13 stars.   Yes   No
4. Now the flag has 13 stars.   Yes   No
5. There is a stripe on the flag for each state.   Yes   No

COLUMBUS DAY: OCTOBER 12 _____

BEFORE YOU READ

Do you know these words?

Europe
Spain
China
India
New World
captain

sailed
fought
thought

Look at a calendar for this year. What day is Columbus Day?
Find Europe on a map. Where is Spain?
Find India and China.
Can you find the New World?
How did you come to this country?

TALK WITH YOUR TEACHER

Who came to America in 1492?
Where was he going?
Who was living here in 1492?

COLUMBUS DAY _____

Christopher Columbus came to America on October 12, 1492. He was looking for a new way to China. The people in Europe liked to buy things from China. Columbus was the captain of three ships, the Nina, the Pinta, and the Santa Maria. He sailed for the King and Queen of Spain. The ships landed on some islands near Central America.

Columbus thought he was in India. He called the people who lived on the islands Indians. He did not know he was in North America. After Columbus, many people came to the New World.

YES/NO

Read the article above. Circle *yes* or *no* after each sentence.

1. Christopher Columbus came to America in 1492.   (Yes)   No
2. Columbus was looking for China.   Yes   No
3. Columbus was from India.   Yes   No
4. America was in the New World.   Yes   No

THANKSGIVING DAY: FOURTH THURSDAY IN NOVEMBER

BEFORE YOU READ

Do you know these words?

Pilgrims
Indians
church
harvest
turkey

farmers
feast
fall
spring

Look at a calendar for this year. When is Thanksgiving Day?
Do you have a special harvest feast in your country? When?
Have you ever celebrated an American Thanksgiving? How?

TALK WITH YOUR TEACHER

Who were the Pilgrims?
Why did they come to America?
Who helped the Pilgrims grow food?
Why did the Pilgrims have a feast?

THANKSGIVING DAY _____

Thanksgiving Day is the fourth Thursday in November. People in the United States visit friends and family on this day. They have a big dinner. Many people eat turkey. On Thanksgiving, Americans think of the Pilgrims and the first Thanksgiving.

The Pilgrims came to America from England in 1620. They did not like the Church of England. They wanted a different church, and they wanted freedom. The Indians were living in America. They were good farmers. The Indians helped the Pilgrims plant and grow corn and other vegetables. In the fall, there was a good harvest. The Indians and Pilgrims had a feast to give thanks. This was the first Thanksgiving.

YES/NO

Read the article above. Circle *yes* or *no* after each sentence.

1. The Pilgrims came to America looking for freedom.   (Yes) No
2. Thanksgiving Day is November 20.   Yes   No
3. The Pilgrims came from England.   Yes   No
4. The Indians helped the Pilgrims grow food.   Yes   No
5. The first Thanksgiving was in the spring.   Yes   No